SCULPTING CLAY

LEON I. NIGROSH

SCULPTING CLAY

DAVIS PUBLICATIONS, INC.
WORCESTER, MASSACHUSETTS

Managing Editor: Wyatt Wade
Associate Editor: Claire Mowbray Golding
Manuscript Editor: Victoria Hughes
Production Editor: Nancy Dutting
Graphic Design: Janis Owens
Photography: Stephen DiRado and Bill Byers
Cover Design: Paola Di Stefano

Front Cover: Jeffrey A. Chapp, *Fruits of Our Labor,* 1988. Slipcast, whiteware, glaze, luster, 14 x 12 x 12″ (35.6 x 30.5 x 30.5 cm). Courtesy: MC Gallery.

Back Cover: Susan Risi, *Love Birds.* Extruded stoneware, oxides, glaze stains, 40 x 26 x 15″ (101.6 x 66 x 38.1 cm).

Printed in the United States of America
Library of Congress Catalog Card Number:
ISBN: 87192-236-3

10 9 8 7 6 5

ACKNOWLEDGMENTS

I would like to express my appreciation to all the artists who took the time and effort to submit examples of their ceramic sculpture for possible inclusion in this book. Photographers Bill Byers and Stephen DiRado deserve a special note for their many hours behind the lens and in the darkroom. Thanks to my studio intern, Todd Lintner, for helping prepare some of the sculpture examples. My gratitude to model Lianne Lally for sitting still for so long. Once again, the staff of Davis Publications deserves mention for helping me with their expertise and encouragement. And finally, I would like to thank my daughter, Maya, for just being my daughter.

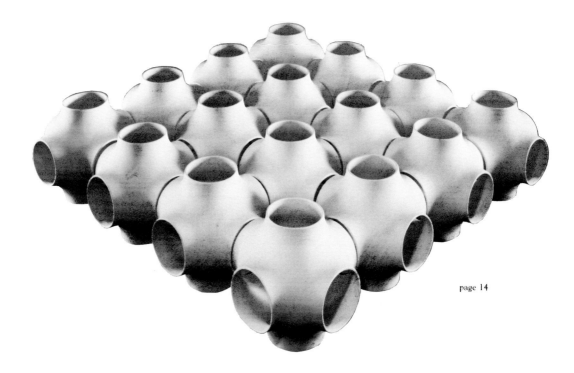

page 14

CONTENTS

page 3

page 53

page 82

page 79

page 132

PREFACE

page 13

From the dawn of civilization humans have mashed, squashed and squeezed clay into objects with which to express themselves. Many of these objects still exist today as reminders of the depths of religious fervor, passion, or simple wonderment people experienced throughout history. Often the greatest strides in art were made during periods of extreme political or social turmoil. The exquisite artworks produced during Japanese feudal times serve as an example of this.

Over the centuries sculptors have been drawn to many materials discovered or developed with superlative qualities of hardness, durability, intrinsic value or scale. Very often, after the initial romance had worn off, sculptors returned to the most basic and natural material — clay.

Initial contact with clay is often haphazard — idle fingering and pushing until some sort of recognizable image appears. If the work is intended to be anything more specific or of greater importance and permanence, certain forming and finishing techniques must be employed. Here is where this book can be of significant value. Starting with basic clay manipulation, each succeeding chapter builds upon the previous one to present techniques logically and methodically. Many picture sequences are presented to give the impression that you are actually performing the process yourself.

Historical and contemporary examples are offered throughout the book to aid in understanding the types of artwork other artists have created using a particular technique. These works can also help stimulate your imagination in developing new ideas of your own.

Suggested equipment needs, along with highly technical information regarding clay body and glaze formulation, have been kept to a minimum. The information which is included is presented in language that is easily understood. (More detailed information can be found in the author's other books: Claywork and Low Fire.) A glossary of terms and raw materials will help identify unfamiliar words or terms. A selection of clay body and glaze recipes is arranged by firing temperature or technique to get you started. Also listed are major manufacturers and suppliers who can provide the necessary ceramic materials and equipment.

Time-honored principles of composition are discussed and illustrated as an aid in developing an overall sculptural sense. As these principles become second nature, their understanding will translate into your own work and each new effort will show qualitative improvement.

Health and safety play an important part in the production of any art form. Awareness of possible hazards and avoidance of them can help ensure a long and fruitful career. A section on health and safety appears in the introduction and cautions and recommendations are written in bold face throughout the text as an aid in reducing potential problems.

page 170

This book was written with the idea that sculpting clay can be both challenging and satisfying at the same time. It is designed to make learning and using ceramic techniques easy so that you might concentrate your energies on the more fulfilling process of creating imaginative sculpture.

SCULPTING CLAY

INTRODUCTION

Highly refined carved jadeite ceremonial figure.
Mezcala culture, Mexico, ca. 10th century.
8 x 2⅝″ (20.6 x 6.7 cm).
Worcester Art Museum.
Gift of Mr. and Mrs. Harold Kaye.

What does "sculpting clay" mean? From deep inside caves and archaeological digs we can find examples of fossilized clay which show the fingermarks of someone from our earliest times who could not resist squeezing and shaping this soft malleable stuff.

The earliest known three-dimensional objects are Old Stone Age artifacts called *eoliths*. These crudely altered stones were used for hammering, scraping and chopping as far back as 500,000 years ago. They were devised as tools for survival, but the subconscious drive to create some kind of object other than the merely useful has always been basic. Humans have continually sought ways to render their world in forms that would be simpler to comprehend. Because clay lent itself to easy manipulation, it was probably the first material to be used for this lofty purpose. The objects that were produced were often endowed with magical powers to aid in such areas as hunting, health and fertility.

With the improvement of various carving and cutting tools, wood became more easily adaptable for artistic purposes. Feeling the need for protection from the dark and other mysterious forces, frail humans surrounded their dwellings and even adorned their bodies with powerful god images made of wood. Unfortunately, few early works of this type have survived. We must rely on the traditional reproduction of these images to gain some idea of their majesty.

Emboldened by their successes in carving wood, artists turned their efforts toward the shaping of stone. As tools improved along with artistic skill and dexterity, the works produced began to have a life of their own. In many cases the works were admired not for their insight, but for their technical expertise.

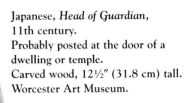

Japanese, *Head of Guardian*,
11th century.
Probably posted at the door of a
dwelling or temple.
Carved wood, 12½″ (31.8 cm) tall.
Worcester Art Museum.

Egyptian, Middle Kingdom, *Offering
Bearer*, 2060–1780 BC.
Carved and painted wooden model.
Worcester Art Museum.

Aztec, *Water Goddess*, 12–13th century.
An example of carved stone with spare
but intricate detail.
13⅜ x 6⅝ x 4⅝″ (34 x 16.8 x 11.7 cm).
Worcester Art Museum.

Left:
Pendant from Panama, Veraguas style, 8th century.
Gold, 2⅞ x 2⅜ x ⅜" (7.3 x 6 x .9 cm).
Worcester Art Museum.
Right:
Greek *Horse*. An example of skill in bronze casting, 8th century BC.
3¾ x ⅞ x 3½" (9.5 x 2.2 x 8.9 cm).
Worcester Art Museum.

As the centuries rolled along new materials continued to be discovered and at each turn, individuals attempted to put their own distinctive mark on them. The development of bronze, an alloy of copper and tin — stronger, more workable and shinier than either, helped metalworkers create grand and fanciful works of art beyond the task of making utilitarian objects. Great strides were also made during the Iron Age when workers, tired of making weapons, poured molten metal into molds of imaginative shapes.

Throughout more recent history, diverse cultures have created magnificent works of art in fine gold. Particularly striking examples still exist which were produced by pre-Columbian peoples in Central and South America.

Today, artists are experimenting with plastics and other modern materials in their attempt to express their personal images of the world around us.

While most of these materials are still in use today as vehicles for

sculpture, they all possess a certain foreboding aura. One cut in the wrong place, and the whole piece is either ruined or has to be altered. Not so with clay. Clay is a most yielding and malleable material. When it is being worked in the wet state, it is very forgiving. Mistakes can be easily corrected, portions can be added or taken off at will.

Sculpting in clay is primarily an **additive** process. That is, more clay can be introduced as needed throughout the entire modeling activity. Works of an architectural scale can be constructed by simply pressing more bits of clay together. Other materials can only be subtracted from or mechanically joined. This is known as a **reductive** process. A large chunk of stone is needed to make a small figure. A piece of wood must first be cut and then somehow pinned, lashed or glued to another before it can become a work of any size. Separate sections of wrought metals must be hammered, bolted or welded to each other for the finished artifact to have any scale.

Left:
An example of a modern material used in a sculpture.
Duane Hanson, *Couple with Shopping Bags*, 1976.
Cast vinyl, polychromed in oils, life-size.
Collection, Morgan Gallery, Kansas City.
Courtesy of O.K. Harris Works of Art, New York.
Photograph: Eric Pollitzer.
Right:
David Smith transformed modern construction materials into works of art. *Cubi XVI*, 1963.
Stainless steel, 33 x 11 x 5' (10 x 3.4 x 1.5 m).
Albright-Knox Art Gallery, Buffalo, NY.
Gift of the Seymour H. Knox Foundation, Inc.

Sculpture can represent one's deep thoughts.
Richard Burkett, *Requiem To A Lost Love*,
1987.
Earthenware, commercial china, 24 x 16 × 16″
(61 x 41 x 41 cm).
Photograph: the artist.

It is the natural organic quality that sets clay apart from all other materials. The sculptor's ideas can be translated through the fingers directly from the brain to the clay. The immediacy of this forming process allows a large measure of spontaneous expression not possible in other media.

Generally, when the word "clay" is mentioned, most people immediately think of utilitarian pottery objects. These works have been produced for centuries and have served well in both their intended use and often as a guide to our historical past. However, by using the same forming methods, materials and finishing techniques, we can take clay beyond the "merely useful" into the realm of imagination. Sculpting clay can go well beyond simple manipulation of a substance to become a physical representation of our deepest thoughts and wildest dreams.

A dream-like installation.
Esther A. Grillo, *Fantasied Garden*, © 1988.
Clay, porcelain, mixed media,
9 x 16 x 9′ (2.8 x 4.9 x 2.8 m).
Photograph: the artist.

One of the benefits of being an artist is having the opportunity to stand back and truly enjoy the fruits of your own labors. It goes without saying that this can best be achieved if you remain healthy and alive. A few simple precautions can insure that you continue to be an active and productive ceramic sculptor. This book can help.

Throughout the text, information related to possible health and safety problems is noted in **bold face.** The glossary offers warnings, also in **bold face,** about the toxic properties of individual raw materials often used in ceramics. Advice about safety masks, gloves and other equipment is offered in appropriate sections of this book.

It is most important to **know the materials** with which you are working. Avoid extremely hazardous substances. Substitute less hazardous materials wherever possible.

Be sure that there is **sufficient ventilation** throughout the studio. Install air inlets and outlets opposite each other so that contaminated air is drawn away from the breathing zone, not through it. Isolate kilns and spray booths and have exhausts vent to the outside.

Keep the studio **clean.** Wipe work surfaces with a wet sponge that is rinsed often. To clean floors, use a wet mop, sweeping compound or a vacuum cleaner with appropriate dust filters and collectors. Dry sweeping only spreads dust around. Microscopic particles can remain airborne for hours after sweeping. Store raw materials in covered containers.

Wear **suitable clothing** in the studio. Keep these clothes for studio use only. Wash them often.

Protect your lungs by using a dust mask when dry mixing clay or glazes. Use a NIOSH approved charcoal respirator when working near fumes and vapors. **Protect your skin.** Wear rubber gloves when wet mixing glazes. Use heat resistant gloves when firing a kiln. **Protect your eyes** by wearing welder's goggles when looking into a hot kiln.

Wash yourself thoroughly after working to reduce chances of absorbing toxic materials.

Do not eat or drink in the studio.
Do not smoke.

1 IDEAS AND PRINCIPLES

In this captivating sculpture Louise Nevelson places disparate elements in harmonious order. *Black Garden Wall III.* 1971.
Painted wood, Formica,
88 x 44 x 7" (223.5 x 111.8 x 17.8 cm).
Worcester Art Museum.

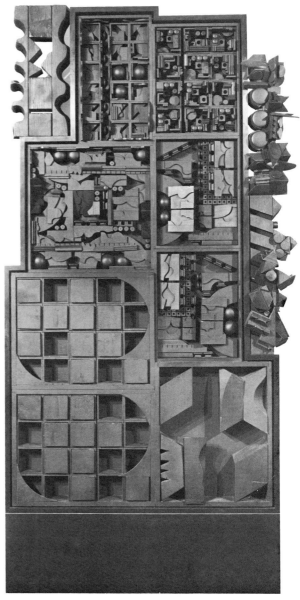

IDEAS

The question most often asked of an artist is, "Where do you get your ideas?" Some artists insist that their ideas are Divine Inspiration. Many claim that the wellspring is their devotion to the Muses. Others cite in-born talent. For most artists, however, the real answer is plain hard work.

STUDY

Ideas come from study: study and understanding of historical as well as contemporary artworks; study of nature and the current world situation; and in-depth study of the materials to be used in creating works of art.

Ideas frequently come from studying the writings of other artists. These autobiographies, and even occasional biographies about particular artists, can lead to direction and insights about one's own work. The recorded musings and notations of artists from centuries gone by can be as fresh as newspaper quotes of living artists. What artists think and how they view life can stimulate new personal ideas or reinforce existing ones.

ORDER

Apparently innate in humans is the desire to have order. The world around us seems chaotic, beyond control. A sense of order needs to be established in one's surroundings — even if it consists of no more than arranging tapes or CDs in alphabetical sequence.

This need for order is invariably the subconscious driving force for many artists. What separates artwork from mere order, however, is the way the artist juxtaposes disparate elements and creates a new harmonious entity. Whether in music, poetry, architecture, sculpture, or other artistic ventures, the most satisfying outcome is one that embodies this concept.

EXPERIMENT

After study comes experimentation. Experiment by developing various three-dimensional forms using the chosen medium. Try other materials and experiment with them to help sharpen an awareness of how things work. Cultivate a sense of curiosity about all things, not just art. Keep notes. Make sketches.

Take the time to develop a real understanding of the chosen medium — in this case, clay. Find out what it can do. Take it to its very limits. The more familiar the clay becomes, the easier it is to make it perform in ways not previously anticipated. Failures are almost as important as successes. By trial and error one can gain confidence in the manipulation of clay and can soon make it do all manner of things. The more practice, the better the results. After a time, handling clay can become almost second nature and earlier problems which appeared insurmountable will seem to solve themselves.

PRINCIPLES OF COMPOSITION

At one time in the not-too-distant past, everyone knew what sculpture was. A sculpture was a bronze statue of a famous war hero astride a rampant horse, a life-sized marble statue of a sinewy Greek athlete clothed only in garland or a fig leaf, or a figure of a demure nymphette with eyes downcast. Suddenly, as if overnight, sculpture seemed to be almost anything: a bicycle wheel, a milk bottle rack, a giant curve of rusting metal. What had happened? Where were the rules?

Artists have always reflected the society in which they lived, recording its tendencies and excesses, sometimes even projecting its future. As todays' society continues to break away from the old rules of politics, religion and social order, art too appears to break from its rules. But is this really the case or has only content changed while basic artistic principles remain intact?

Marcel Duchamp, *Bicycle Wheel*, 1951 Metal and wood, 50½ x 25½ x 16⅝ (128.27 x 64.77 x 42.21 cm) Collection, The Museum of Modern Art, New York. The Sidney and Harriet Janis Collection.

Nineteenth century Italian carved marble statue of *Cupid and Psyche* (after Antonio Canova). Worcester Art Museum. Gift of Mr. and Mrs. Joseph E. Davis.

Below left: Thomas Crawford, *Boy Playing Marbles*, 1853. Marble, 27¾ x 31 x 15⅝" (70.5 x 78.7 x 39.7 cm). Worcester Art Museum. Bequest of Stephen Salisbury III.

PURPOSE

Although not technically a principle of composition, the overriding component necessary in a sculptural work must be its purpose or intent. Why create a sculpture in the first place? The idea being expressed has to stimulate the viewer. Whether a work is abstract or figurative, it can tell a story, display some political position or simply evoke an emotion. However, if it fails to catch and hold the viewer's attention, the work cannot be considered a success.

BALANCE

Beyond the technical necessity of being able to stand upright, a ceramic sculpture must have visual balance or equilibrium. This can be attained by placing equal masses or appendages physically and visually in opposition to each other. Areas of light and dark color or varying textures can also help provide a sense of balance within a work.

Balance can also be achieved asymmetrically in a work by arranging smaller forms around the visual axis so that their "weight" counters that of larger masses. If appropriately executed, asymmetry offers greater dynamic excitement than does symmetry.

A work certain to command attention.
Jack Thompson (AKA Jugo de Vegetales, *Madre Coneja*, 1987.
Clay, stucco, 73 x 20 x 16″ (108.4 x 50.8 x 40.6 cm).
Photograph: the artist.

This figure displays visual balance because its elements are arranged equally.
Parvati. Southern India. Cast bronze, 19⅝ x 7½ x 6⅞″ (49.9 x 19 x 17.5 cm).
Worcester Art Museum.

A work in asymmetrical balance. Don Pilcher, *Eulogy Vase Series*, 1987. Clay, enamel, mixed media, 16″ (41 cm) tall. Collection: Mr. and Mrs. Michael Brillson. Photograph: W. Zehr.

This sculpture maintains its balance through the use of both equal element placement and color change. Martha A. Holt. *Woman Tree #4*, 1987.
Glazed earthenware, 38 x 16 x 13″ (96.5 x 41 x 33 cm).
Photograph: Mark Perrott.

PROPORTION

The satisfactory size relationships among the parts of a sculpture help to convey a sense of order. While ancient Greeks worked out rules of proportion mathematically, most artists work intuitively with a sense of what feels right. The idealized proportions of the human body are often the basis for this understanding. Even untrained viewers have this innate sense of "rightness" and apply it to everything they encounter. An artist may also choose to exaggerate the proportion of all or part of a work to express an idea. Whether the size relationships of a piece are idealized or exaggerated, proportion is an important part of its visual effect.

An abstract vision of a human endeavor with proportions that "feel right."
Susan Eisen, *Navigator*, 1988.
Lowfire clay, mixed media, 15½ x 18 x 3″
(39.1 x 45.7 x 7.6 cm).
Photograph: George Ancona.

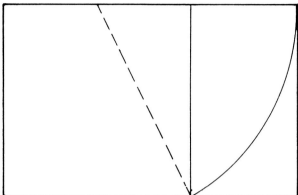

Construction for Golden Rectangle.

UNITY, REPETITION AND VARIETY

To best express the intent of a sculpture, all its parts must come together as a unified whole. The textures, colors, planes and spaces need to work together to express the theme of the work forcefully. However, if all of these elements are uniform in visual interest, the work can be stagnant and boring.

Repeated forms within a sculpture can be of different sizes or textures that still successfully relate to each other. Repetition does not necessarily mean duplication, although in some cases this too can be effective.

A sculpture can be brought to life by varying the characteristics of the elements that go into its composition. Incorporating an occasional shocking or disparate form can serve well to enliven an object. Too great a diversity, however, can lead to confusion and diminish the impact of the work.

A sculpture with a unified theme.
Kazuko K. Matthews,
Clay Sculpture.
Stoneware,
65 x 7 x 9″
(165.1 x
17.8 x 22.9 cm).
Photograph: Susan Einstein.

Duplicated forms are effectively used in this sculpture by
Harriet E. Brisson. *Schwarz Surface.*
Slipcast whiteware, each unit: 12 x 12 x 12″
(30.5 x 30.5 x 30.5 cm).
Photograph: Bob Nash.

The spacing of the slabs makes the clay appear
to be climbing the wall.
Valerie Bowe, *Modulation No. 3*, 1986.
Unglazed terra-cotta, 34 x 16 x 62″
(86.4 x 40.6 x 157.5 cm).
Photograph: Karen Mauch.

The incorporation of neon in this work heightens
the visual impact. Richard Burkett, *Twisters*, 1989.
Earthenware, mixed media, 113 x 93 x 99″
(2.9 x 2.4 x 2.5 m).
Photograph: the artist.

RHYTHM AND MOVEMENT

The interaction of rhythm and movement are more subtle aspects of
composition. The arrangement of size, color and textural relationships
of the parts of a sculpture direct the viewer's gaze over and around the
object. Successfully executed, the sense of movement will draw the
viewer deeper into the nuances of the sculpture and increase the interest and appreciation of the work. (It has been recorded that museum
visitors spend an average of less than ten seconds looking at an individual artwork.)

The mood of this sculpture is made more enigmatic through the use of repeated forms in different sizes. Elizabeth MacDonald, *Untitled*. Low-fired stoneware, 10 x 11 x 7″ (25.4 x 28 x 17.8 cm). Photograph: Bob Rush.

To what end does abiding by these precepts lead? In the classic age of sculpture, any deviation from these principles led to expulsion from exhibition and banishment from the world of **art haut.** Today, many sculptors appear to ignore the concepts altogether and still meet with great success in the opinion of both critics and galleries.

Upon closer examination of notable contemporary clay sculptures, however, it can be seen that it is really only the content, the ideas expressed, that has changed. Competent execution, technical skill, and proper use of the principles of composition still play an important role in the development of a sculpture of fine quality. But, rather than to simply please viewers, the emphasis is to make them think and maybe even act.

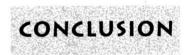

CONCLUSION

An artistic statement to make the viewer think about what will become of the residue of today's mass production. Katherine L. Ross, *Vessels in the Landscape,* 1988. Slipcast lowfire clay, chain link fence, 24 x 24 x 14″ (60.1 x 60.1 x 35.6 cm). Photograph: the artist.

2 WHICH CLAY?

An installation using various amounts of clay set in water and left to dry.
Valerie Otani, Elizabeth Stanek, Andreé S. Thompson, *Clay in Change* (view of drying edge), 1984.
Slip, sand, adobe, native clay, fired as found, 25 x 30′ (7.6 x 9.1 m).
Location: Walnut Creek Civic Art Gallery, Walnut Creek, California.
Photograph: Andreé S. Thompson.

The choice of clay depends upon the ultimate disposition of the finished work. Clay can be dug from the ground and used with only a little preparation. Certain clays can be mixed so that the finished work can be displayed without the need for firing. Modeling clays can be made to stay moist and not harden. Other clays may need to be fired at different temperatures depending upon the need for weather resistance.

NATURAL CLAY

Digging and processing one's own clay can be an exciting and integral part of the entire sculpture activity. Prospecting for local clays — each with its own particular variations — can enhance the inner qualities of the finished piece. Clayworkers in many cultures search for special clays, keep their whereabouts a secret and impart magical attributes to these clays.

Workable clays can be found at riverbanks, quarries and places where the topsoil has been removed such as road cuts or building sites. Most clays found in this manner are known as **earthenware.** While appearing in their unfired state as green, yellow, brown or black in color, they generally fire a reddish-brown to black.

ON-SITE TESTS

Several simple tests can be performed on-site to determine if the clay is usable. Roll a sample of the clay into a coil about the thickness of a pencil and wrap it around a finger. If there are few cracks, the clay is plastic and will hold its shape.

Set a piece of clay aside to dry. If a whitish scum forms, the clay contains alkalies. Alkalies can reduce the workability of the clay and cause the clay to slump when fired. However, alkalies can be removed from the clay during the washing stage of preparation.

The presence of lime in the clay may be harmful during firing. Lime particles expand when fired and could cause unwanted craters in the finished work. To test for lime, drop a small sample of the clay into a 50 percent solution of hydrochloric acid. **Hydrochloric acid is highly corrosive, wear rubber gloves.** If bubbling occurs, too much lime is present and the clay is not usable.

Small amounts of other impurities such as sand, twigs and rocks can usually be screened from the clay.

PREPARING THE CLAY

If the on-site tests show the clay to be usable, take a 5 pound (2.27 kg) sample back to the studio, break it into small pieces and let it dry completely. Next, crush the clay as finely as possible and pass it through a 60-mesh screen to remove any granular debris. Pour the clay into a container of water and stir vigorously. After several hours siphon off the top water. This action removes alkalies and unwanted organic matter without losing any fine clay particles. Add more water and repeat the process every few hours until the top water is clear. Then siphon off all the water and pour out the clay onto drying bats or on another clean surface. Allow the clay to set up, or begin to dry, until it is almost stiff. Ball up the clay and store it in an airtight container for at least a week. This will allow the clay time to **temper,** or age, to somewhat improve its plasticity.

CLAY BODIES

Although many clays taken directly from the ground can be used to make and fire sculpture, they often do not have the necessary characteristics some sculptors desire. Most single clays do not have the proper color, wet strength, plasticity or fired density to be practical for a sculptor's needs.

By mixing two or more clays together along with various chemicals and fillers, the required effects can be produced in what is known as a clay body. In order to do this properly, a working knowledge of the chemical and physical properties of the many raw materials is needed. Fortunately, myriad clay bodies are available from ceramic suppliers and at least one will probably have attributes close to those desired.

TESTS FOR CLAY

After a clay is chosen, either from the ground or from a catalog, three important tests should be performed to fully understand its capabilities.

WATER OF PLASTICITY

Plasticity is the indicator of the workability of the clay. If the clay is too sticky it will not hold a shape. If it is too "short," or non-plastic, it will break apart while being formed.

When working with dry powdered clay, it is necessary to determine the water of plasticity, the amount of water needed to make the clay workable. Fill a 100 cc (cubic centimeter) graduated cylinder with water. Add small amounts of water to 100 grams of powdered clay until the mixture has become workable. Record the amount of water used. Then add more water until the clay is sticky. Record this amount. This test gives the range of water content needed to make the clay usable.

If the clay comes moist from a bag, simply use the coil wrapping test noted earlier.

SHRINKAGE

Shrinkage occurs at several stages. The clay first shrinks as it dries and the water of plasticity evaporates. Clay shrinks again when it is put through the first, or **bisque,** fire as the chemically combined water is driven out. The final, and often the most extensive, shrinkage happens during the final firing when chemical compounds that make up the clay begin to fuse. Knowing the amount of shrinkage can be very helpful when developing a sculpture that must be a certain size when finished. Shrinkage that is too great will cause warping, cracking or deformation of a clay object. Too little shrinkage indicates that the clay has not properly vitrified.

To test for shrinkage, make several bars of clay, 13 cm (centimeters) long, 4 cm wide and 1 cm thick. Draw a line exactly 10 cm long on each bar. Allow them to dry between lightweight plaster bats or wooden boards to prevent warping. When the clay bars are dry, measure the line with a centimeter ruler. Subtract this measurement from 100 mm (the original measurement) to get the percentage of dry shrinkage. Fire the bars to the maturing temperature of the clay and measure the lines again to determine the total shrinkage.

Natural shrinkage rates vary from 10 to 25 percent. Clays that shrink 12 to 15 percent are considered good.

POROSITY

Porosity is the measure of vitrification, or amount of water absorption, of a fired clay. Knowing the absorption rate of a clay can help determine its resistance to the elements. The less porous a fired clay is, the less water it absorbs. This reduces the chances of freezing and cracking in colder climates and helps prevent **spalling** or splintering, caused by internal water pressure in warmer climes.

To test for porosity, separately weigh the unglazed, fired clay bars and record their weights. Boil the bars in water for at least two hours. Remove the bars, blot them and immediately weigh each of them again. Calculate the absorption as follows.

$$\frac{\text{Saturated Weight} - \text{Dry Weight}}{\text{Dry Weight}} \times 100 = \text{Percentage Absorption}$$

Earthenware clays generally have an absorption rate of 4 to 10 percent; stoneware clays, 1 to 6 percent; and porcelains, 0 to 3 percent. Adjusting fluxes or firing higher can reduce porosity and make the clay more vitreous.

These tests should be performed on all clay bodies before they are put to use.

KNEADING

For best results, clay should be well homogenized and free of air bubbles before it is put to use. Kneading is the simplest way to prepare small amounts of clay.

To knead clay, use a sturdy canvas-covered table 30 to 32 inches (76.2 to 81.3 cm) tall or, for a large mass of clay, kneel on the floor. First pat an appropriate amount of clay into a ball. Place the ball on the table and then push it out of round with the palms of both hands. Keep the arms straight and use the shoulders and back to provide pressure. Next, lift the far end of the clay with either hand and give it a quarter turn up and over the forward edge, toward the body. Bring the

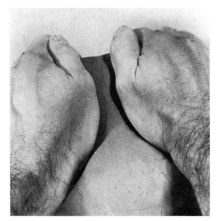

When pushing the ball of clay out of round with both palms, be sure pressure is even.

Bring the clay back up with a quarter turn and repeat using a rhythmic motion.

A spiral shape will result if kneading is properly done. Pat the spiral into a ball before use.

other hand back to the clay and push down and away with even pressure from both palms. Repeat this process using the same hand to lift each time. If done properly, the clay will form into a spiral exposing a changing surface which allows any air bubbles to break open as the clay becomes evenly homogenized. Merely rolling the clay will keep the air trapped causing difficulties later. With a rocking motion of the body, continue to knead the clay until it has an even, workable consistency. Then pat the clay into a ball shape.

If the clay is too soft, continue kneading. The canvas will absorb moisture during the process. If the clay is too stiff to knead easily, slice it thinly and stack it with alternate layers of softer clay, and knead it all to a workable plasticity.

As work on a sculpture progresses, bits and pieces of clay are often cut away or otherwise discarded from the object. Left exposed to air, this clay will soon become too hard for use. Rather than throw the clay away (an expensive and wasteful proposition) one of several methods can be employed to make the clay reusable — to reclaim it.

RECLAIMING CLAY

To reclaim small amounts of clay, have a bucket of water nearby. At the end of a session, crumble up all the discarded bits of hardened clay and throw them into the water. The clay will soon **slake** down into a thick slurry. When the bucket has become full, stir the slurry and let it settle. Pour off the standing water and scoop out the clay onto a drying bat and let it stiffen. Knead the clay and bag it for later use.

To reclaim solid chunks of clay, they must first be allowed to become completely dry. Crush the chunks with a mallet before dropping them into the water. Whole lumps of clay thrown into the bucket will not slake down, but will remain hard, making kneading difficult.

PUG MILL

Large amounts of clay are more easily reclaimed using a **pug mill.** The action of this machine is similar to a meat grinder. It mixes, grinds, kneads and compacts the clay into a workable consistency. Clay that has been stiffened on drying bats can be passed through a pug mill fairly rapidly to make it workable. Soft and stiff clay can be thoroughly mixed together. Water can be added to dry clay scraps as well. Some pug mills have attachments that remove the air from the clay, further compacting the clay and improving its consistency.

Pug mill.
Courtesy Peter Pugger

CASTING SLIP

Dry scraps of casting slip can be reclaimed by adding them to batches of new slip. Because this can upset the balance of deflocculant, such additions should be kept to less than 10 percent. A tiny amount of sodium silicate can be added to maintain the correct balance, but this can often render the slip less usable. Most slip manufacturers, for obvious reasons, do not recommend this procedure. For practical purposes it is probably wisest to thoughtfully dispose of small amounts of dry scrap.

NON-FIRED CLAYS

The preceding information is primarily for clays which will eventually be fired. There are several types of clays that sculptors might find useful that do not require firing.

OIL-BASED CLAYS

Natural clays require water to make them plastic and usable for sculpting. If left to the elements, the objects would eventually crumble and decay back to their original state, as either sticky or dry clay. Firing is required in order to make the sculptures permanent.

Natural clays and clay bodies can be used to create objects to be cast in other materials or as **maquettes,** small models of works to be enlarged. The major drawback to using these clays for modeling is that they must be kept constantly moist or they will become too dry to be worked.

Clay compounds mixed with oils and waxes will remain soft and workable indefinitely. Therefore, this type of modeling clay is usually the sculptor's choice for making master objects for later casting. Many brands are readily available from clay suppliers and come in different colors and degrees of firmness. The colors are mostly for fun, but the varied grades of stiffness are important. Softer clays are more pliable and easier to use for hand modeling. Harder clays are best suited for detail work involving the use of tools.

After the project has been completed, the object can be torn down and the clay stored in a covered container for later use.

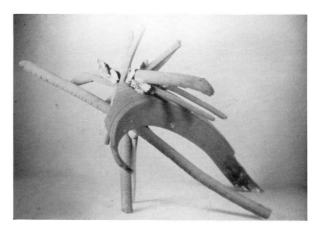

Clay maquette for larger work.

Sydney K. Hamburger, *Fragsus*.
Welded steel, 72 x 96 x 104" (1.8 x 2.4 x 2.6 m).

SELF-HARDENING CLAYS

This type of clay sounds like a dream come true. Just make something and let it dry — no kiln needed. In truth, these clays are usually a commercial mixture of natural clays, fillers, hardeners and glues (trade secrets all!) which when left out in the air will harden without crumbling. Some of these clays can be made a bit sturdier by "oven firing" to about 350°F (176.7 C).

The major drawback to self-hardening clay is that it is just that. If left untended for too long a period, the entire supply can become irreversibly hard. Because self-hardening clay is generally not very responsive to the touch and is relatively expensive as well, it is probably best used for small models or simple design exercises.

Above left:
Natural clay maquette to be translated into bronze.
Phyllis Baker-Hammond, *Seven Ages*.
Clay, 18 x 7 x 6" (45.7 x 17.8 x 15.2 cm).
Photograph: Lee Bolton.

Joyce Kohl, *Untitled*, 1988.
Adobe, paint,
2 x 1½ x 1' (61 x 45.7 x 30.5 cm).

ADOBE

Adobe has been used for centuries to house people the world over. It is simply sun-baked earth. Properly prepared adobe is a good material for use in creating large outdoor sculpture.

Certain soils are better for making adobe than others. Soils with high kaolin content and which contain coarse sand work best. Avoid beach sand because the salt content can weaken the structure.

Tests for Adobe

Dig a sample of local soil and let it dry. Crush it and screen out all pebbles and organic material. Place a handful of soil into a jar of water and shake until thoroughly mixed. Let the mixture settle. When the water is clear, the clay content should appear to be between 25 and 45 percent of the mixture; sand and silt between 50 and 75 percent. Too much clay will make the adobe shrink and crack when dry. Too much silt and sand will make the adobe crumble. Add whichever ingredients are necessary to achieve the proper balance.

Adobe will not stand the rigors of weathering for very long. The addition of 1 to 6 percent of emulsified asphalt will stabilize adobe and make it waterproof. Make small brick samples of each amount and allow them to dry for 24 hours. Then break each sample in half. The one that does not crumble, but breaks with sharp edges is best. Soak each sample in water for several hours. Properly stabilized samples will not crumble or cloud the water. Several formulas may prove successful. Of these, choose the combination with the least amount of emulsified asphalt. When adobe has reached stabilization, additional asphalt has no effect. Portland cement in amounts up to 20 percent can be used as a stabilizer instead of emulsified asphalt. The adobe may be stronger, but not as waterproof.

Adobe can be used in press molds, applied to wood and wire frameworks or shoveled in a heap and modeled into the desired form.

Joyce Kohl, *Adobe House Displaced*, 1986.
Adobe, paint, 3 x 20 x 20' (.9 x 6.1 x 6.1 m).

Upon opening any ceramic supply catalog, one discovers a vast array of clay bodies — all, according to the text, capable of working wonders. It is therefore necessary to decide which of these compounds will be best suited for a proposed work.

While color and texture might be the most important features that come to mind, it is really the firing temperature that is of primary importance. Sculpture that is to be placed outdoors must be constructed of high temperature clay impervious to weather conditions. Works that will contain liquid should be built of vitreous clays that are waterproof. Forms that will not have to withstand rough handling can be made from low temperature clays. Objects to be viewed from behind glass cases can be fired just enough to harden them.

Based upon the ultimate disposition of the sculpture, determine a temperature which will provide the required results. Once the firing temperature has been decided upon, examine the products offered within that range. Accept the catalog explanation of each clay at face value, then obtain samples of several possible choices. Review and perform the tests for clay earlier in this chapter before selecting a particular clay and embarking on an important work.

LOWFIRE CLAYS

Low temperature, or lowfire, clays are considered to be those that are relatively mature when fired within cone 08 to cone 02 (945° to 1101° C/1733° to 2014° F).

Earthenware clays are the most abundant and available of natural clays and clay bodies. Their fired colors range from red-orange through tans and browns to metallic black. The color depends upon how "contaminated" the clay is with various iron oxide compounds. The greater the iron content, the darker the color. Unfortunately, the more iron that is present, the less vitrified the clay will be when fired. Therefore, most earthenware clay is not suitable for outdoor sculpture.

Natural earthenwares vary in plasticity from sticky to grainy and accordingly are more or less satisfactory for the production of sculpture. Commercial bodies have been formulated so that they usually are well suited to all building materials. **Terra-cotta** is a commonly available type of earthenware body that, because of its plastic quality and rich textural effect, is appropriate for sculpture. It is commercially available in a wide range of colors, from brick red to chocolate and black, and can be purchased with or without coarse or fine grog.

FIRED CLAYS

Chinese, *Horse*, T'ang dynasty (5th–9th century). Terra-cotta, 26¼" (66.6 cm) tall. Worcester Art Museum.

Sometimes after earthenware has been fired, an unpleasant whitish **efflorescence,** or scumming, appears on its surface. This occurs because calcium sulfate (present in most clays) has not been properly decomposed by firing. Adding a small amount of barium carbonate to the clay body will counteract this situation.

Whiteware refers to a type of light-colored or white clay body fired at a low temperature. It is usually composed of kaolin and other high fire white clays with large amounts of nonclay materials, such as talc and feldspar, added to lower firing maturity. These additions render the clay somewhat less plastic than other earthenwares, but most hand-building techniques are not affected. In fact, sculpture made from some talc bodies can be built quite thick or solid. If fired very slowly, they will not crack or break. However, as usual, testing is recommended.

Bill Stewart, *First Pueblo*, 1989.
Glazed terra-cotta, 56 x 20 x 18"
(142.2 x 50.8 x 45.7 cm).
Photograph: Earl Cage (Museographics).

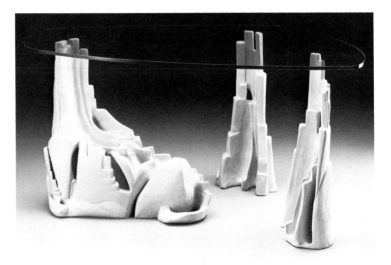

Judy Motzkin, *Castle* (pedestal table), 1988.
Glazed whiteware, glass, 26 x 36 x 36"
(66 x 91.4 x 91.4 cm).

A fantasy board game — "nonfunctional for us, good for the spirits in Tut's tomb."
David B. Ward (Camelman 1364 BC),
Necropoly Game. © 1984.
Low-fired porcelain, glaze, glaze stains, dye transfer, 22 x 22 x 4" (55.9 x 55.9 x 10.1 cm).

STONEWARE CLAYS

Naturally occurring **stoneware** clays mature within a temperature range of cone 5 to cone 12 (1177° to 1306° C/2151° to 2383° F). They can fire from buff and tan to grey and brown in **oxidation firing,** and toasty orange to black in **reduction firing.** The color depends upon the amount and kind of "impurities" present in the clay, such as iron or manganese, which also affect the plasticity and vitrification of the clay. Most stoneware clays are quite plastic, have a long firing range and low porosity when fired. These qualities make stoneware an excellent clay for sculpture which is to be placed outdoors or in water.

Commercial stoneware bodies are available in a broad spectrum of colors and textures and are generally a good choice for sculpture.

PORCELAIN

Porcelain does not occur naturally, but is a type of clay body usually composed of high fire china clay (kaolin), ball clay, and other materials. When fired to a temperature of cone 12 (1306° C/2383° F) or above, it produces a hard vitreous, translucent white body. Commercial porcelains that can achieve similar results at lower stoneware temperatures are available.

Porcelain is far less plastic than stoneware and is therefore somewhat more difficult to manipulate. It has a "memory," or tendency to return to its original shape and will often warp during firing. Given these minor disadvantages, all the forming techniques can still be used successfully to create detailed sculptural works.

Because most sculptural works are not necessarily concerned with food safety or the ability to retain liquids, any of the foregoing clays can be fired below their effective maturing temperatures and still be relatively sturdy and damage resistant — with the exceptions stated.

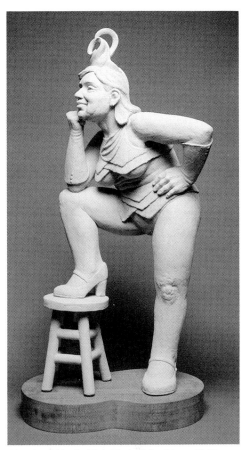

Claudia Olds Goldie, *End of the Line*, 1982. Stoneware, paint, 31″ (78.7 cm) tall. Photograph: David Webber.

Kathryn Besley, *The Two of Us Again*, 1985.
Matt-glazed porcelain,
8¼ x 10 x 3½″
(21 x 25.4 x 8.9 cm).
Photograph: Allan Laughmiller.

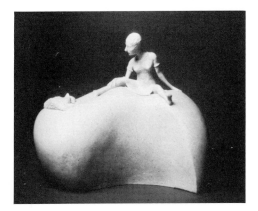

ADDITIVES

Adding organic material, such as coarse sawdust, to the clay can help increase the wet strength of the clay, reduce shrinkage and control warping. When the clay is fired, the material burns away leaving the sculpture lighter in weight. Grass clippings, rice hulls and coffee grounds are other organics often used. **Grog,** prefired ground-up clay, can be added to the clay to help give greater wet strength and reduce shrinkage. But, it does increase the fired weight. There are practical limits regarding how much grog can be added. A 10 to 20 percent addition by weight is acceptable. Greater amounts of grog will make the clay **short,** and more difficult to manipulate.

Expanded mica granules, used for home insulation purposes, can be introduced into the clay in amounts up to 10 percent. This material aids in reducing shrinkage and warping. It also does not burn-out in firing, but leaves gold-like flecks in the clay.

One or two percent of chopped nylon fibers added to clay will form a matrix which makes it easy to build paper thin walls. The nylon combines with the clay when fired to produce a more durable object. The use of nylon fiber is not suitable for wheel throwing.

COLORED CLAY

As an alternative to glazing, colored clay can be directly incorporated into ceramic sculpture to provide attractive effects. Colored clays can be used at all temperatures and atmospheres when appropriate colorants are used.

A pronounced color can be given to clay by adding coloring oxides or commercial stains (1 to 15 percent by weight). Best results are achieved with a white or light colored clay body since clays can be made darker in color, but not lighter.

Copper carbonate and chrome oxide give good green colors with additions of 1 to 5 percent. Iron oxide can darken a clay with as little as 1 percent and turn it red-brown with a 3 to 5 percent addition. This oxide will stain everything it touches, however, so use it judiciously. Manganese dioxide or rutile can be used to make brown colors, but both must be used in much higher percentages. Cobalt will easily tint a clay blue with as little as ½ percent addition. Follow manufacturers' recommendations when using stains. Too much colorant can flux a clay body and cause it to melt when fired. Make test samples of each color to be certain of the results.

A whimsical clay bugle that can actually be played.
Stephen C. Smeed, *Bugle.*
Wheel-thrown, inlaid colored clay.
Photograph: Alfonzo the Great.

To add colorant to small amounts of clay, poke a hole in a ball of clay and sprinkle in the colorant along with a few drops of water. Thoroughly knead the clay until the colorant is fully dispersed. With larger amounts of clay, it is best to dry mix all the ingredients before adding water. Keep the clays separate and use different canvas or plaster when kneading each color to prevent contamination. **Wear rubber gloves to protect the hands.**

Take care not to muddy the colors when working on a form. If necessary, carefully sandpaper or scrape the object after the clay has dried to restore color definition. Do not wash with a damp sponge — this only worsens the condition.

Fire the work with a clear gloss glaze for brightest results. Softer colors will show through some semi-matt glazes. Even without glaze, colored clays can enhance a fired work.

Elizabeth MacDonald. *Wall Piece.*
Stoneware, pressed-in powdered pigments, 30″ (76.2 cm) diameter.

A portion of a 450 square foot (137 sq. m) floor mural made of colored clay tiles executed by local school children.
Elee Koplow, David Judelson, *Hurley Street Playground Mural* (detail), © 1981.
Inlaid colored stoneware.
Commissioned by the Cambridge Arts Council, Cambridge, MA.
Photograph: Marc Malin.

3 HANDFORMING

Warren Hullow, Isabel Parks, *SeaForm I*, Stoneware,
10 x 19 x 19″ (25.4 x 48.1 x 48.1 cm).
Photograph: Bobby Hansson.

The only elements necessary to begin sculpting in clay are some clay and one's hands. Take a wad of clay and pat it, bang it, slap it or squeeze it from one hand to the other. Really feel the clay. Sense how it feels against the skin. Note how it reacts as it stiffens and warms with use. Examine the clay to see if grog sticks out. Does it always stay smooth? Is it too slimy or too stiff to work with? See how thin the clay can stretch before it cracks. Simply manipulate the clay with no purpose other than to become familiar with it.

GEOMETRIC SOLIDS

The painter Paul Cézanne (1839–1906) believed that all of nature could be reduced to geometric forms: cylinders, cubes, spheres and cones. Try testing Cézanne's theory with the following experiments.

1. Roll a wad of clay between both hands to make a sphere. Smooth it so that there are no lumps. Continue to make balls of clay until "perfect" spheres are attained.

2. To form a cube, gently tap one of the spheres on a tabletop. Now make another one with really sharp edges and corners. Keep trying this until accurate cubes emerge.

3. Roll a small wad of clay on a table and tap each end to form a cylinder. Again, continue to do this with different pieces of clay to make the best cylinders possible.

4. By rolling and tapping, work some clay into a solid cone. Repeat these actions to make several precise cones.

Sculpture made of different size fired clay spheres.
John Rossetti, *Terri's Balls*, 1985.
Low-fired stoneware, paint, wood,
14 x 14 x 3½" (35.6 x 35.6 x 8.9 cm).
Collection: Terri Priest. Photograph: Ron White.

An assortment of clay spheres.

A group of solid cubes.

Small rolled cylinders.

A collection of cones made in various shapes.

When a group of small geometric pieces has been collected, select one piece and position it on top of another. Join the two together, deforming them as little as possible. Notice how the forms relate to each other. Pay particular attention to the manner in which they connect. Keep the edges sharp and the individual pieces smooth and regular. Make a series of joined pieces.

Try to create a visual compression between the parts and give them a feeling of weight. Assemble other pieces to give a feeling of extension and weightlessness. Do any of the assembled pieces have a hint of human appearance? Try to construct a small figure using various geometric parts.

Solid forms joined in a simple composition.

Forms assembled to show extension and lightness.

Geometric pieces assembled to suggest a human form.

Forms joined to convey the impression of weight.

Geometric sculpture portraying a moving figure. Umberto Boccioni, *Unique Forms of Continuity in Space*, 1913. Bronze, 43⅞ x 34⅞ x 15¾″ (111.5 x 88.6 x 40 cm). Collection: The Museum of Modern Art, New York. Acquired through the Lillie P. Bliss Bequest.

Human-like sculpture formed by altering solid blocks of clay.
Tom Schottman, *Repose*, 1989.
Stoneware, oxides, 20 x 12 x 30″ (50.8 x 30.5 x 76.2 cm).
Photograph: George Mastellone.

FREE FORMS

Squeezed and modified organic forms.

Take a handful of clay and gently squeeze it. Smooth away edges and rough areas without severely altering the form. Manipulate the piece until it fits comfortably in the hand. Make a series of objects in this manner allowing the initial squeezing to dictate the final form. Imagine the look and feel of ocean-tumbled stones.

One of the major aspects of sculpture is the play of light and shadow over a form. Keep this in mind while working. Hold the form in different positions to see what highlights and shadows occur. Accent ridges and depressions to create a sense of movement throughout the form using light and shade.

How do these forms differ from the geometric solids? Can the free forms be assembled in interesting ways, or does their interest lie in their individuality?

An assemblage of organic forms.

HAND MODELING

Choose an appetizing fruit or vegetable such as a banana, green pepper, pear or squash. Model this in solid clay using only the hands. Pay special attention to any crevices or protrusions. Use water sparingly while modeling the form, moistening the fingers on a damp sponge rather than wetting the clay. Make the piece as lifelike as possible. Remember that the model has a bottom as well as other views.

Green pepper modeled by hand only.

Doing the foregoing exercises by hand helps gain an understanding of the ways clay can be manipulated. The advantage of direct touching is rare with most other sculpting materials. Stone carvers must use a hand mallet and chisel or pneumatic chisel to work hard stone. To sculpt wood, a pocket knife must be used or even a chain saw. Once a comfortable rapport between hands and clay has been established, tools can then be employed for what they really should be — extensions of the hand.

MODELING WITH TOOLS

Try sculpting another version of the same fruit or vegetable. This time use simple loop tools, paddles and knives as needed. Compare the outcome with the hand modeled version. Is one a more accurate representation than the other or is one more "artistic"?

Using a tool to sculpt another pepper form.

CARVING

Up to this point the exercises have all been done by modeling the basic form and building up or modifying its surface. This time start with an appropriately sized solid block of well-kneaded clay. Examine the model fruit or vegetable. Then, using a knife or loop tool, simply cut away all the clay from the block that does not look like the model. Not as easy as it sounds. Imagine if the block were not clay but marble and a mistake is made. Once a piece has been cut from the block it cannot be replaced.

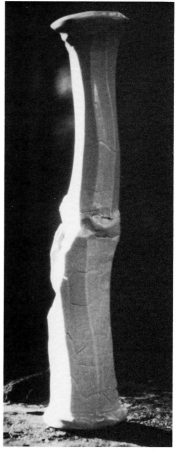

A solid carved sculpture.
Dennis Parks, *Silesian Column VII.*
Porcelain, glaze, 18″ (45.7 cm) tall.
Photograph: the artist.

Stone and wood sculpting employ reductive techniques, removing unwanted material to slowly bring about the desired results. Although carving, or cutting away, may be appropriate to some work in clay, the vast majority of clay sculpture can be performed by using various additive modeling or building techniques.

A sculpture composed of both geometric and organic forms.
Calvin Albert, *Bridge*.
Solid terra-cotta, unglazed,
18 x 18 x 13″
(45.7 x 45.7 x 33 cm).
Photograph: Martha Albert.

HOLLOWING FORMS

To make clay objects permanent they should be fired. Generally, to avoid problems later, the walls should be no thicker than ½ inch (1.27 cm) in cross-section. Therefore, objects which have been modeled solidly must be hollowed out. Cut the form in half and carve out the interior until the walls are the proper thinness. Then secure the two halves by roughing the edges to be joined, coat them with vinegar and press them together. Vinegar is a very mild acid which softens clay more rapidly than plain water or clay slurry. Weld the seams, adding bits of clay if needed, and smooth the surface. Be sure to make a hole somewhere in the form to allow steam to escape during firing. Otherwise, pressure will build up and the piece will explode in the kiln.

To avoid all the extra work of hollowing a finished form, works can be made with one of several hollow building techniques. The simplest method is **pinch forming.**

Take a ball of clay in the palm of one hand. Insert the thumb of the other hand into the clay almost all the way to the bottom. Lightly pinch the wall with the thumb and fingers while slowly rotating the ball. With little effort a pinch form will appear. By holding the thumb and fingers in different positions, varied textures can be made. Experiment with the size and shape of the ball when pinching. Make tall narrow pieces and forms with open or closed rims.

If the clay starts to crack because pinching is drying it out, occasionally moisten the fingertips on a damp sponge. Do not put water on the clay. This will just make a soggy mess. If the clay does get too wet, put the piece aside until it has stiffened before trying to continue.

PINCH FORMS

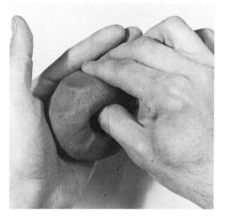 

Pushing a hole in the center of a clay ball.   Lightly pinching the clay walls.

MULTIPLE FORMS

After making several open forms, assemble them into larger freestanding objects. Accent the concave quality in some pieces. Feature the convex aspect in other works.

Abigail Sarah Hannaford, *Pinch Figures*, 1989. Unglazed earthenware, each figure: 3½″ (8.9 cm) tall. Photograph: the author.

Assembled concave pinch forms.

Pinch forms assembled to feature their convex aspect.

MIXED FORMS

Construct and combine hollowed geometric and organic forms to develop more complex sculptures. Introduce textures to further heighten the contrast between the geometric and organic parts. Try using similar elements from one composition in another, but change the sizes. Often, by working on a series of sculptures, ideas develop more rapidly than when working with just one piece. Quick sketches of the proposed idea can help resolve problems of joining as well as composition.

Remember that air must be able to pass through all parts of the hollow form. Be sure to put holes in each section of the form to prevent explosions later.

Author, *Figure*, 1989.
Pinch-formed stoneware, oxides,
5½ x 4 x 2″ (14 x 10 x 5.1 cm).

Right:
Joanne Redman, *Creature Piece*, 1989.
Glazed whiteware, underglazes,
7 x 3 x 3″ (17.8 x 7.6 x 7.6 cm).

Sketch of proposed sculpture showing support placement and shrinking slab.

Sometimes it is necessary to use props to support parts of the sculpture during construction and drying (and in some cases, firing). Make the supports from clay. This will allow them to dry and shrink along with the sculpture, preventing damage to the work in progress. It is helpful to include the placement of the props in the original idea sketches.

Although it is possible to use massive blocks of clay to carve and bigger chunks to pinch, it soon becomes obvious that there are practical limits to size. Other methods of hollow building and construction such as coil and slab building are more suitable for larger clay sculptures. Chapters four and five cover these methods in detail.

Large sculpture made of pinched forms.
Ruth Aizuss Migdal, *Venus #1–87*, 1987.
Stoneware, epoxy, oilstick, wax,
45 x 30 x 20″ (114.3 x 76.2 x 50.8 cm).
Photograph: the artist.

Christine B. Knox, *Succulence #20*, 1987.
Porcelain, acrylic paint,
32 x 14 x 13″ (81.1 x 35.6 x 33 cm).

4 COILBUILDING

Coilbuilding is historically the most popular method of composing sculpture in clay. Almost every culture, from ancient times to the present, has used this method to create hollow forms of almost every sort imaginable. Because the building method itself has a certain organic quality, the vast majority of coil-built work has been figurative. The early Mayans, the Etruscans and others, readily recognized the ease with which coils could be made to represent human and animal forms. Today, although coils are still used in making figures, many sculptors prefer to explore the asymmetrical and organic aspects of the method and develop imaginative abstract forms.

A contemporary abstract figure built with large coils.
Robert Pulley, *Tipper*.
Stoneware, oxides, once-fired in reduction,
43 x 22 x 16″ (109.2 x 55.9 x 40.6 cm).
Photograph: Wilbur Montgomery.

Coil-built *Warrior Figure* from Totonac culture, Mexico,
15th century.
Painted terra-cotta,
16¾ x 10¼ x 5¾″ (42.6 x 26 x 14.6 cm).
Worcester Art Museum.

MAKING THE BASE

Regardless of the final form intended, the basic method of coilbuilding is the same. First, flatten a piece of well-kneaded clay and model it into the shape of the desired base. For most works, a base need be no thicker than ½ inch (1.27 cm). Smaller objects can have a thinner base and larger ones, thicker within reason. Too thin and the base will crack, too thick and it will explode in firing. For ease in handling, place the base on a plaster or wooden bat on top of a bench wheel.

MAKING A COIL

Squeeze out a rope of well-kneaded clay evenly with both hands. Place the rope on a table and roll it back and forth with light, even pressure. Keep the hands level with the tabletop and roll with the full length of the fingers and palms. To start, roll the clay from the center outward. As the coil lengthens, continue to roll evenly from either the center out or from the ends inward. Keep rolling until the coil is the proper thickness, depending on the size of the intended sculpture. Quick, short strokes with only fingers or palms will make uneven lumpy coils. Some practice may be needed in order to make coils that are satisfactory.

When building larger forms, or if a smoother surface is required, use wide coils. Roll out a large diameter coil and then flatten the entire length by tamping with the edge of the hand. In this way the height of the coil is increased while maintaining the appropriate width.

Forming the base for a coil-built piece.

Squeezing out a coil rope.

Rolling a coil with long, even strokes.

JOINING

After a proper coil has been rolled, flatten one end and press it directly on top of the perimeter of the base until the ends overlap. Seal the inside seam by moving clay vertically with a finger or wooden tool. Smooth over all the sealing marks. In this way a firm join can be assured and drying cracks avoided. Continue to roll and attach each successive coil in the same manner. It is not necessary to roll an extremely long coil to fit the entire rim of an object. Overlap the ends of workable lengths of coil and join to complete the distance.

There is no particular saving gained by stacking many coils before sealing the interior. By joining each coil completely before adding the next, it becomes easier to maintain control of the final form.

The first coil is placed on top of the base near the edge.

Sealing the coil to the base with a wooden tool.

The interior is sealed and smoothed.

Placing a coil on the outer edge to widen the form.

BUILDING

Before starting to develop large or complex sculptures, draw several sketches to be certain of the form wanted. Show dimensions, note any joints or fittings, indicate where supports should be placed if needed. Sketching will also help organize the manner in which the sculpture can best be put together. Often, sculptures can be more effectively realized by constructing them in sections to be joined after the clay has stiffened. Appendages can also be made separately and secured to the main body when the clay has set up, preventing possible collapse.

To build a form that swells out, place each coil toward the outer edge of the preceding coil. In some cases, large diameter bowl-shaped parts are best built upside down. Adding coils from the widest diameter up and inward distributes the weight of the clay more evenly and is less likely to collapse than if the clay were cantilevered outward. When stiff, the form can be turned upright and joined with other parts.

To constrict a form, place each coil on the inner edge of the coil below. If the diameter of the work appears to be getting too wide, cut several darts (small wedges) from the rim. Bring the rim together, score the cut edges and seal everything firmly.

As the sculpture progresses upward, it is a good idea to paddle each coil down to help insure a firm join. A paddle can also be used to define the form as the clay sets up.

Scoring and wetting the coils before joining is only necessary after the clay has begun to set up. Roughen the top of the stiffened coil with a hacksaw blade or other serrated edge and brush on vinegar.

TEXTURES

The marks of the fingers or wooden tools used in the simple act of joining the coils can often create a pleasant surface texture quite natural to the form. Other textures can be produced by roughing the outside surface with a toothed scraper or splintered stick. Various objects such as dowels, bolts or twigs could be used to stamp textures into the clay. Use rope- or burlap-covered paddles to develop texture while firmly joining the coils at the same time. Build in decorative texture by making swirls, dots and waves from the coils or by merely varying their heights.

Smooth surfaces can be easily obtained by first scraping the area with a serrated edge to even out imperfections and then working the area with a rubber or wooden kidney. Resist the temptation to smear the area with water. This can soften the clay too much and cause collapse.

This large coil sculpture was built in one piece.
Brian Buckley, *Yahday*, 1985.
Stoneware, paint,
108 x 24 x 24″
(274.3 x 61 x 61 cm).
Photograph: the artist.

A highly textured surface enhances this coil-built sculpture.
Robert L. Glover, *Fasia/Fasciatus*.
Unglazed lowfire clay,
53 x 24 x 4″ (134.6 x 61 x 10.2 cm).
Courtesy of Space Gallery.
Photograph: Susan Einstein.

A smooth surface on this work magnifies the softness of the curving forms.
Charles C. Katinas, Jr., *Torso #5*.
Stoneware sealed with 50/50 Elmer's Glue-All and water, 30 x 20 x 20″ (76.2 x 50.8 x 50.8 cm).

CONTROLLED DRYING

As clay is exposed to air it begins to dry. When working on large sculptures it is necessary to keep the finished portions of the work from drying too soon. The best way to control this is to wrap plastic around these areas so that they will stiffen but not dry. To keep an unfinished piece workable, lightly mist it with water from a spray bottle before wrapping it in plastic. This allows the moisture content of the clay to equalize while it is in storage.

If a work or a part of it has become completely dry, there is essentially no way that the clay can be adequately softened or new clay added. Soaking the piece in water or dousing with vinegar may seem to soften the clay, but cracks will continue to appear as it dries. When fired, the added clay will break away.

It is important that completed sculptures be allowed to dry slowly and evenly. Daily wrapping and unwrapping with plastic will help keep drying at a steady pace. Drying time will vary with studio temperature and humidity. If some areas of the work appear to be drying faster than others, keep them covered until the rest of the piece is as dry. Coating thin edges or other rapidly drying parts with **wax resist** will slow drying by blocking moisture release. Remember that each joint in a work is a potential crack·in drying or firing.

Coil-built sculpture, illuminated from below.
Author, *Future Man*,
Glazed stoneware, Acrylite, luster,
6 x 3 x 2′ (1.8 x .9 x .6 m).
Private collection, Long Island, NY.

Mimi Okino, *Bivalence*, 1983.
Stoneware, steel,
23 x 30 x 14″ (58.4 x 76.2 x 35.6 cm).
Photograph: Little Bobbie Hanson.

PATCH CONSTRUCTION

This method is a variation on standard coilbuilding. Instead of rolling long coils of clay, just flatten pieces of clay into patties and then join them in the usual manner. The varied shapes of the patches create an attractive natural surface texture.

Large clay patches were used to build each form for this installation.
Tova Beck Friedman, *Goddesses*, 1988.
Unglazed stoneware, oxides,
tallest figure: 5′ 5″ (1.7 m)
Photograph: Tim Volk.

Small clay patches were used to construct this sculpture.
Maybelle Kou, *Freddy*, 1989.
Unglazed whiteware, oxide,
13 x 12 x 8″ (33 x 30.5 x 20.3 cm).
Photograph: the author.

Bailey Standard 4 Extruder.

EXTRUDERS

Clay extruders operated by hand or machine can be used to produce a virtually endless supply of coils with less effort than hand rolling. Most extruders can be fitted with a series of dies of various sizes ranging from string thickness to four or five inches in diameter. Dies can also be fashioned to extrude grooved or flattened coils. If extensive work with coils is intended, an extruder would be a worthwhile investment.

See Chapter 5 for an explanation of how extruders can be used to produce hollow forms.

5 CONSTRUCTING WITH SLABS

An example of a wall mural made of large slabs.
Dale Zheutlin, *Cycloid*.
Low-fired porcelain, stains,
14 x 6' x 5" (4.3 x 1.8 m x 12.7 cm).
Private residence, NJ.
Photograph: Paul Warchol.

Slabs, or sheets of clay, can be used in many ways to create a variety of sculptural forms from small low-relief tiles to large free-standing architectural works.

Because a slab is nothing more than a flattened piece of clay, it can be made easily by beating a lump of clay with the fist. The resulting shape might be acceptable for certain works, but its uneven thickness and lack of internal structure could cause problems in drying and firing. Cutting the slab with wire, a method preferred by Far Eastern clay-workers or rolling the clay with the pizza method, both help to create slabs of even thickness and consistency.

CUTTING

Place the wire in the bottom slots of two sticks that have equidistant notches cut in them. Stretch the wire tightly and then pull it through a squared block of well-kneaded clay. Set the wire into the next notch and repeat the process, raising the wire a notch for each pass.

MAKING A SLAB

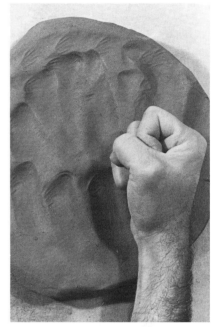

Flattening a slab with the fist.

Using notched sticks and wire to cut a block of clay into slabs of even thickness.

ROLLING

First thoroughly knead a ball of clay. Next, flatten it somewhat by batting it with the fist. Lift the clay up by its farthest edge. Without letting go, flip it up and downward against a tabletop or floor with a pulling motion, allowing the far end of the clay to touch first. Repeat the process by taking the far edge of the clay, lifting and dropping it down away from the body and pulling it back with a swinging motion. To control the width, alternate these movements by grasping the clay by a side edge and slapping it down. Continue to perform these actions until the slab is slightly thicker than needed.

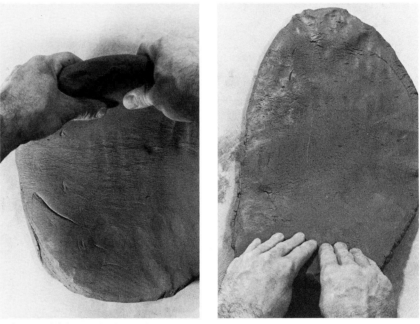

Lifting a slab by its farthest edge.   **Pulling the clay as it hits the table.**

   Next, place the slab on the floor on top of a piece of canvas or other heavy fabric. Put two guide sticks (i.e. yardsticks) on either side of, but not touching, the slab. Cover the clay and sticks with another piece of canvas. Set a large pipe or rolling pin across the middle of the clay and guide sticks. Stand on the pipe and roll it to one end. Put the pipe back in the center and roll to the other end. By using the entire weight of the body, this method is less tiring than rolling slabs by hand. If there are ripples in the clay, or if it has not been leveled to its proper thickness, peel off the top piece of canvas and flip the slab onto it. Separate the other piece of cloth from the clay, reset the guide sticks, replace the canvas and roll again.

The thickness of the guide sticks depends on the size of the sculpture to be built. Most slab works can be safely fabricated with walls between ³⁄₁₆ and ¾ inch (.16–1.9 cm) in thickness. Thicker slabs do not necessarily make a sculpture stronger. If the clay is too thick it can cause uneven drying, construction cracks, and explode when fired.

Very large slabs can be rolled by taking several smaller slabs and overlapping their edges. Paddle down the clay, weld the seams and roll the joints flat.

To make immense slabs for wall panels or murals, lay out the clay in reasonable widths, leaving spaces for the guide sticks. Roll the slabs in the usual manner. Force clay into the spaces and hammer it down to the proper thickness.

Several high-quality slab rolling machines are commercially available. The major advantage to these machines is that they are capable of quickly rolling large-sized slabs of even consistency and thickness without much effort on the part of the sculptor. However, they are relatively expensive and require proper maintenance. The size of the slab that can be rolled depends upon the width of the rollers and the space between rolling surfaces. In some cases the length of the slab is restricted by the size of the rolling platform.

AMACO Slab roller, model T-2.

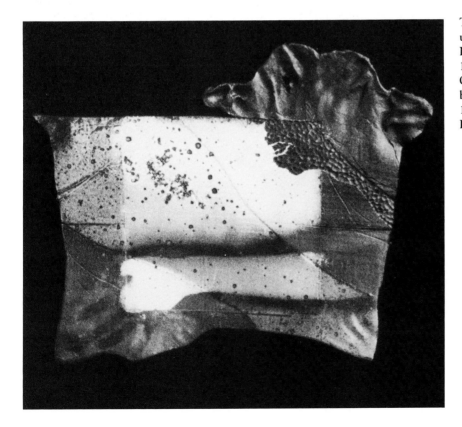

This wall panel was made by cutting and unfolding a wheel-thrown cylinder.
Dennis Parks, *The Descent To Malbolge,* 1987.
Once-fired stoneware, vapor glazed in oil-burning kiln,
18 x 22″ (45.7 x 55.9 cm).
Photograph: the artist.

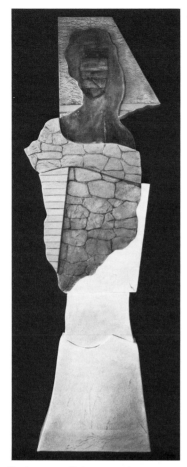

Sculpture utilizing carved textures.
Richard Moquin, *Figure 4, Ostia Antica*, 1982–1983.
Unglazed earthenware, body stains,
74½ x 25 x 13¼"
(189.2 x 63.5 x 33.7 cm).

TEXTURE

The natural texture of the canvas or burlap used for slab rolling can be enhanced by rolling the clay on other materials such as shag rugs, netting and lace. Other textures can be achieved by laying objects such as random lengths of string, leaves, bits of cardboard or wire mesh onto the clay and rerolling the slab. After rolling, remember to remove the objects from the clay. Still other surfaces can be produced by lightly beating the slab with carved rope-wrapped paddles, meat tenderizing mallets or sticks.

OTHER CONSIDERATIONS

To help prevent distorting the slab after it has been rolled, peel off the top canvas and turn the slab onto it. Take off the other cloth before beginning any cuts. After careful measuring, cut the slabs to size with a knife, and let the slabs stiffen. If the slabs must be stored for later use, stack them one on top of another with several sheets of newspaper in between. The paper absorbs moisture and helps dry the clay evenly. If the slabs must be kept soft, just stack them together without the paper. Wrap the entire stack in plastic and place everything on a board for easy transportation.

Fanciful sculptures with impressed textures.
Jillian Barber, *Standing Goat Figures*, 1987.
Glazed whiteware, lusters,
24" (61 cm) tall.
Photograph: Martin Doyle.

Slabs can be used when they are either soft or stiff. To make flat-sided, box-like works the clay must be allowed to stiffen. Other objects can be made while the clay is still soft.

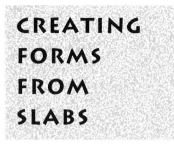

Louis E. Mendez, *Post-Modern Antecedent*, 1988.
Incised earthenware, glaze,
33 x 24 x 11″ (83.8 x 61 x 27.9 cm).
Photograph: Ralph Gabriner.

Debra Trager, *Bird Horse*.
Stoneware, airbrushed glaze stains,
23 x 22 x 12″ (58.4 x 55.9 x 30.5 cm).
Photograph: Ralph Gabriner.

BAG FORMS

Soft-looking, puffed-up objects like birds, animals and monsters can be formed by wrapping clay around crumpled newspaper.

Placing newspaper wad inside a folded clay slab.

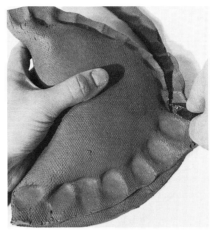

Trimming sealed bag form.

After a slab has been rolled out, place loosely crumpled newspaper in the center. Lift one end of the slab over the paper, press it onto the other part of the slab and firmly pinch the clay all around. Trim off the excess clay. Experimentation with different dimensions and amounts of paper can lead to unlimited images. Combine varied sizes in a grouping, add different appendages, stack several forms together.

After the work has been completed, it must be allowed to dry slowly. If it is possible to remove the paper before firing, do so, otherwise the paper will burn in firing and the ash can be shaken out later.

CYLINDERS

Cylinders can be made in different sizes and dimensions. They can have appendages, be placed in different positions, presented singly, stacked, or combined with other geometric or organic forms.

Above:
A work emphasizing the cylinder.
Mary Lou Alberetti, *Column*.
Glazed whiteware, glaze stains,
oxides, underglazes,
21 x 6 x 4″
(53.3 x 15.2 x 10.2 cm).
Photograph: Jim Cordes.
Right:
This outdoor sculpture by Valerie
Bowe was made primarily from
cylinders. *Formation No. 2*, 1986.
Unglazed stoneware,
10 x 96 x 24″
(25.4 x 243.8 x 61 cm).
Photograph: the artist.

Cylindrical shapes can be made easily while clay slabs are still soft. Wrap a cardboard mailing tube with several sheets of newspaper to prevent the clay from sticking. Lay the tube on the slab and gently roll the clay over it. Firmly press the edges together. The join marks may act as decoration, or, if a smooth join is preferred, bevel the edges of the slab before sealing. To close the bottom, stand the tube upright onto another slab and cut around it. Seal this cap to the cylinder. After the clay has set up somewhat, remove the mailing tube and newspaper. If the tube remains inside the cylinder too long, the shrinking clay will either have gripped the tube too tightly to remove or, worse, will have split. Be sure to seal the inside seams of the cylinder and finish the rim by smoothing, cutting or tearing.

If the cylinder is to be closed, simply invert it onto the slab, cut another cap and seal the joint. To insure secure joints, paddle the entire form. A small hole must be poked through the slab somewhere to prevent explosion when the capped cylinder is fired.

Cutting away excess clay at the base of the cylinder.

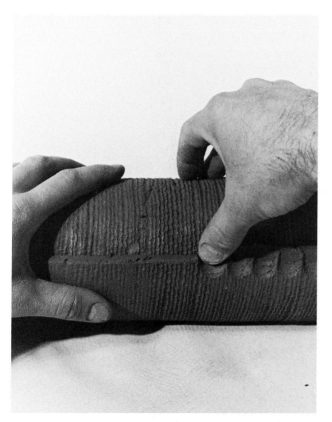

Sealing a slab around a mailing tube.

USING MOLDS

Simple dish shapes can be produced by pressing soft slabs into a shallow baking tin. Line the tin with strips of newspaper to keep the clay from sticking. Deeper shapes can be made by draping slabs over paper covered inverted bowls.

Two molded slabs can be joined to make an enclosed form. Score the edges, apply vinegar and join the parts together. Add thin coils to fill the seams and paddle everything to create secure joints. Be sure to poke a hole through the clay somewhere to prevent explosion in firing. Attach appendages to the form, assemble it with similar forms or combine it with other geometric or organic parts. A greater discussion of the use of plaster molds can be found in Chapter 10.

Floor sculpture made from press-molded slabs.
Vladimir Petrov (Moscow, USSR).
Glazed chamotte (terra-cotta),
6′ (1.8 m) long.
Photograph: Joseph Bennion.

Pressing a slab into a shallow pan.

Measured slabs ready to be assembled.

BOXES

Flat-sided, sharp-edged geometric forms can be best fabricated from stiffened slabs of clay. After a suitable slab has been rolled out and allowed to stiffen somewhat, cut carefully measured pieces from the slab and let them become firm but not leather hard. Next, bevel those

Scoring the beveled edge of a slab.

Joining two slabs using a wooden tool.

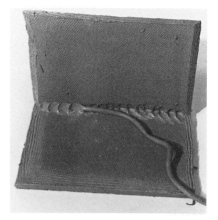

Sealing the joint with a thin coil.

edges to be attached at 45°. This increases the joining area and hides corner seams. Score all the surfaces to be joined and coat them with vinegar. Stand one side piece on top of the base and join the two by welding the inside seam using a finger or wooden tool. Add a narrow coil to the joint and smooth it in for a firm seal. Smooth the exterior of the join and paddle it to assure strong adhesion. Continue to add sides in this manner until they are all securely attached to the base and to each other. Score the top edges of all the side slabs, as well as the joining area of the top and apply vinegar. Set the top slab in position and join it to the exterior. Paddle all seams and edges to insure solid joints and sharp corners. Do any additional decorating, carving or squaring while the box is still sealed. The trapped air inside will prevent the box from becoming deformed.

To make a box into a covered container, slice around the upper portion of the sides. For a level cut, measure upward from the table at each corner and draw a line. After the box is open, seal the interior joint of the top. Make a flange to keep the cover on by attaching a thin strip of clay to the inside top of the walls. Replacing the cover and allowing both parts to dry slowly together helps to reduce warping. If the box is to remain closed, a small hole must be poked through somewhere to prevent explosion in firing.

Flat-sided slab forms do not need to be cubes. Three sided forms can be made in the same way. The beveled angle has to be changed from 45° to 60°. Multisided forms can also be produced by adjusting the angle of the joint accordingly.

Measuring box prior to cutting cover.

Attaching flange to interior of box.

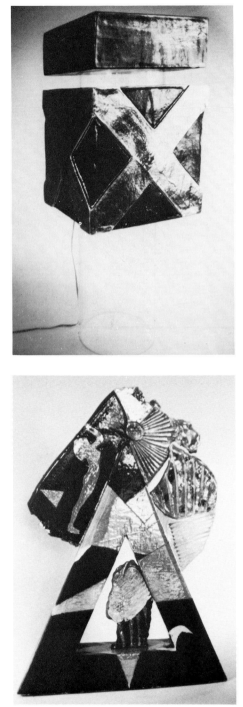

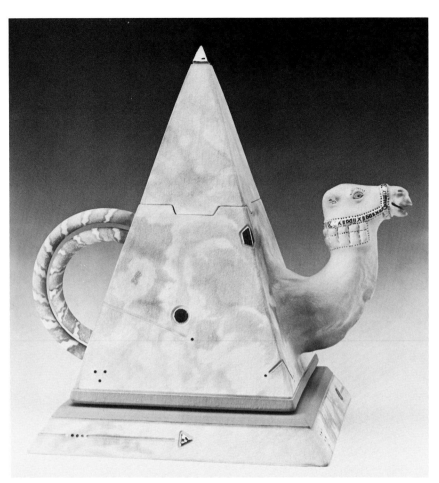

A pyramidial work made from slabs.
David B. Ward (Camelman, 1364 BC). *Teapot,* © 1986.
Glazed whiteware, lusters, dye transfer,
8 x 8 x 12″ (20.3 x 20.3 x 30.5 cm).
Above left:
Slab-built sculpture illuminated from within.
Author, *Ex Luminus.*
Glazed stoneware, luster, Acrylite,
30″ (76.2 cm) tall.

A slab sculpture with 60° angles.
John DiCicco, *Molecular Wind.*
Glazed stoneware, lusters,
24 x 18 x 4″. (61 x 45.7 x 10.2 cm).
Photograph: Akio Yasuhara.

PATTERNS

To construct complex forms with varied parts or many similar sides, first make full-sized paper or cardboard patterns. By carefully measuring and cutting these patterns, a great deal of time can be saved when cutting the actual clay slabs. Proper angles, joints and any needed supports can also be determined in advance.

The nature of slab construction makes large-scale sculpture fairly easy to fabricate. As the slabs get larger, however, certain technical problems could arise. The dangers of uneven drying, warping and cracking are increased as the slab size is extended. Considerable added weight can sometimes cause difficulties in transportation or display of finished works. To control uneven drying, warping or cracking and to reduce fired weight, add 10 to 20 percent of expanded mica or organic materials such as sawdust or grass clippings. Similar amounts of grog can be used to achieve the same purposes but will not reduce fired weight.

Noncoated fiberglass cloth can be used to give slabs greater tensile strength when plastic. Make the slabs by dipping the cloth into thick slip **deflocculated** with a small amount of sodium silicate or Calgon. Deflocculation neutralizes the electronic charges of the clay molecules. The molecules will no longer clump together, but will remain separated in suspension. Otherwise the clay will break away from the cloth upon drying. The slab thickness is determined by the number of dipped cloths layered together. When fired, the fiberglass combines with the clay. **Wear rubber gloves to prevent possible rash or cuts.**

LARGE-SCALE CONSTRUCTIONS

A group of large scale slab-built sculptures. Phyllis Baker-Hammond, *Caryatids*, 1987. Partially glazed stoneware, 8 x 2 x 1¾' (2.4 x .6 x .5 m). Photograph: Howard Goodman.

One view of the completed sculpture. Irene Wheeler, *Beirut No. 5*. Three different unglazed stonewares, 27 x 32 x 42" (68.6 x 81.3 x 106.7 cm). Photograph: Kathleen O'Reilly. Right: One of several pages of working drawings for a sculpture by Irene Wheeler.

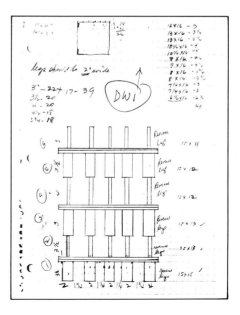

A sculpture made from thick solid clay slabs.
Bruno LaVerdiere, *Black Temple*.
Stoneware, body stains, steel,
49 x 19 x 6″ (124.5 x 48.3 x 15.2 cm).
Photograph: Joseph Levy.
Above right:
Large sculpture assembled from smaller units.
Marilyn Lysohir, *The Dark Side of Dazzle
(Ship)*, 1986.
Earthenware, terra sigillata, wood,
9 x 24 x 4¼′ (2.7 x 7.3 x 1.3 m).
Photograph: Susan Einstein.

SOME CONSIDERATIONS

Large slabs can safely be somewhat thicker than smaller ones and therefore must be allowed to stiffen and dry more gradually.

Elaborate armatures and complex interior braces are not needed if care is taken during each step of construction. To prevent slabs from slumping, it is often practical to construct a form on its side or longest dimension and allow it to dry in this position. If possible, bisque fire the piece in the same position.

The use of a clay **shrinking slab** is advisable to prevent a complex sculpture from warping or cracking during drying or firing. Make this slab at the same time as the sculpture and it will dry and shrink at the same rate. By placing the work on top of the slab, the base will be protected from distortion.

When building with large slabs, bow the sides and top slightly outward to help prevent the sucked-in look some slab objects have after firing. This phenomenon occurs because the outside surface and edges of a slab dry faster than the interior, causing concave warping.

Be sure to paddle all seems vigorously to ensure good strong joints. Paddling will also help fine tune edges.

TILES

To make individual tiles it is helpful to first make an actual size sketch of the proposed design. Roll out a slab of well-kneaded clay from ¼ to ½ an inch (.65 to 1.27 cm) thick. Stamp, cut, carve or model the composition to completion.

Allow the tiles to stiffen until they are almost leather hard. Carve a waffle pattern on the back of each tile. This effectively reduces the weight of the tiles when fired. It also provides more extensive surface edges to grip if the tiles are to be adhered to another material. Cut deeper into the reverse of any thicker areas so that the tile thickness is even throughout. This cutting will permit the tiles to dry more evenly and reduce warping as well. If possible, keep turning the tiles over, to assist with even drying.

Relief tiles can be produced and duplicated by using press molds. See Chapter 10.

LOW-RELIEF TILES AND PANELS

Stamping decoration into a soft clay tile.

Carving a waffle pattern in the reverse of the tile.

Left:
A free-standing sculpture made of thinly rolled tiles. Patricia Beglin, *Threaded Spindle Piece*. Pit-fired porcelain, linen thread, 6 x 4 x 4″ (15.2 x 10.2 x 10.2 cm).

A colorful wall panel in low relief.
Barbara Grossman Karyo, *Contemplation*.
Whiteware, underglazes, glaze stains, terra
sigillata, 18 x 18″ (45.7 x 45.7 cm).

PANELS

If a panel must fit within certain measurements, first draw the design taking shrinkage into account. If the clay has a 10 percent shrinkage after firing, make the drawing 10 percent larger.

Roll a slab of the proper size and thickness. Trace the drawing directly onto the clay with a dull-pointed stick or pencil. When the panel has been totally modeled, cut the clay into pieces of manageable size. For greater visual interest, make cuts along the lines of the composition instead of cutting regular grid portions. When the clay is almost leather hard, waffle cut the back and carefully dry the pieces.

SETTING TILES

To be certain that fired tiles will remain securely attached to a wooden board, the board must be clean, uncoated and have a roughened surface.

Of all the adhesives currently on the market, silicone sealer has thus far proved superior for ease of handling as well as strength. GE Silicone II is excellent for attaching fired clay to wood, metal, plexiglass and untreated sheet rock. It is available in large tubes which fit a standard caulking gun. **Follow the precautions on the label** and then squeeze out a bead of sealer over the entire back of a tile and put it in place with a twisting movement. Continue to do this with each tile until the whole panel is in place. The set up time for the sealer is relatively short, so make every effort to work quickly but not carelessly.

Some tile setting mastics are also acceptable for certain installations. However, most cannot accept the weight of handmade tiles mounted in a vertical position. Try a test sample before using any of these materials on an important project. The advantage to using silicone sealer or mastic instead of epoxy glues or cement is that they do not become completely hard or brittle. This allows the sealer to expand or contract with normal temperature changes and prevents the tiles from splitting or falling off.

ARCHITECTURAL MURALS

Architectural murals are most exciting when clay is used in high relief. The play of light and shadow over an otherwise flat wall can create a visual and emotional appeal.

A wall panel constructed in layers.
Dale Zheutlin, *Thirlmere*.
Low-fired porcelain, glaze stains,
74 x 24 x 5″ (188 x 61 x 12.7 cm).
Commission: Kramer, Levin, New
York. Photograph: Paul Warchol.

The procedure in fabricating a large scale work is similar to the procedure for wall panels. A full-sized cartoon of the work should be made
large enough to take final clay shrinkage into consideration. If the mural is to have deep modeling, prepare slab sections 2 to 3 inches (5.1 to
7.6 cm) thick. This is easily accomplished by slamming fistfuls of clay
onto a canvas covered floor. Hammer the clay with a large paddle or
mallet to prevent air pockets. Next, roll out the clay to be sure it is
level.

Section of mural piece showing area left for better adhesion.

Trace the drawing onto the clay. While modeling the surface, keep sections not being worked covered with plastic. Occasionally mist water on the entire piece to keep the clay workable.

After the mural has been satisfactorily modeled, allow the clay to set up. Cut the work into manageable pieces. To facilitate even drying, hollow each piece overall to a thickness of about ⅜ inch (.95 cm). Leave a rim on the underside of each piece at least 1 inch (2.54 cm) wide to provide sufficient surface area for adhesive.

If the mural is to be permanently installed, lay up a mortar bed of even thickness on the wall. Fill the cavity of each piece level with **neat cement** or commercial dryset mortar. This provides a greater bearing surface to each section when set into the fresh mortar. For work to be put up in a public place, check local building codes to be certain that required installation procedures are followed. Hire professional masons to be sure.

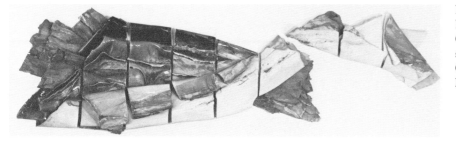

Large mural for a public space.
Elise Gray, *Sky Mountain (Section II)*, 1987.
Glazed white stoneware, underglazes, glaze stains, 6 x 39′ (1.8 x 11.9 m).
Commission: IBM Corporation, Gaithersburg, MD. Photograph: Stacy Duncan.

Maria Alquilar, *Whale Mural*, 1987.
Glazed stoneware, underglazes, glaze stains, china paints, 4 x 10′ (1.2 x 3m).
Commission: Water and Sewer Administration, Sacramento, California.

Clay extruders can be used to produce a diversity of hollow forms for sculpture. Large diameter barrels or boxes can be fitted to extruders so that whole sections of a work can be made at one time. Die kits with simple shapes are available from extruder manufacturers. If these shapes are not adequate, design and cut specific contours from sheet metal, plywood or thick plexiglass. Bevel the edges of the cuts to ensure smooth extrusions.

For most work, mount the extruder vertically. Tightly clamp the selected die to the extruder. Load the extruder with clay and pull the handle to squeeze out the shape to the desired length. When starting the extrusion, hold a board at the mouth of the machine so the clay shape is resting on it. As the clay is extruded, lower the board simultaneously. This action allows forms of considerable length to be produced with a minimum of handling and little warping. Cut the extrusion with a knife or wire and put it aside to set up. After the clay has stiffened, assemble the sculpture with the usual methods.

Extruders, fitted with appropriate dies, can also be used to make flat or relief tiles. In this case, mount the extruder horizontally so that the tiles can be extruded directly onto boards, thus reducing handling and warping.

EXTRUDED SCULPTURE

Commercial wooden extruder die.

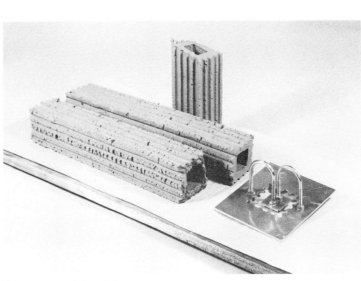

Metal extruder dies, both commercial and studio fabricated.

Extrusions and fluted die.

Extruding a hollow fluted form.

This glass-topped *Column Cocktail Table* was
made from fluted extrusions.
John J. Murphy III, 1989.
Raku-fired glazed stoneware,
21 x 50 x 20″ (53.3 x 127 x 50.8 cm).
Photograph: the artist.
Below right:
An extruded sculpture.
Susan Risi, *Modern Primitive Man*.
Stoneware, paint,
36 x 20 x 12″ (91.4 x 50.8 x 30.5 cm)
Photograph: Ralph Gabriner.

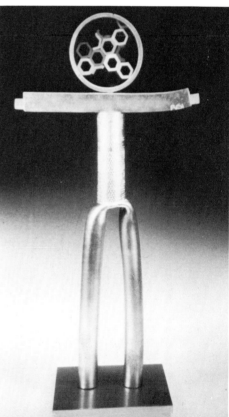

Chairs were constructed of extruded parts to make
this piece.
Katherine L. Ross, *Salt House/Hair House*, 1983.
Reduction-fired stoneware, salt, stainless steel, horsehair,
40 x 20 x 72″ (101.6 x 50.8 x 182.9 cm).
Photograph: the artist.

Several different dies were used to extrude parts for this sculpture. Robert Milnes, *Diamond Jack*, 1986. Glazed earthenware, lusters, 26 x 14 x 9" (66 x 35.6 x 22.9 cm). Collection: Federal Reserve Bank, Cleveland, Ohio. Photograph: the artist.

6 WHEEL-THROWN SCULPTURE

When one thinks of work done on the potter's wheel, the images that come to mind are usually vessels and containers — objects that have been successfully produced for millenia. However, if the wheel is considered as simply another tool in the sculptor's studio, a wide range of forms can be envisioned.

Wheel-thrown garden sculpture.
Zeljko Kujundzic, *Native Girl*.
Glazed stoneware,
28″ (71.1 cm) tall.

THROWING TOOLS

Aside from a wheel that runs smoothly and true, all that is needed are a few basic hand tools. To apply or remove water during throwing, use a thin natural sponge, preferably an **elephant ear sponge.** Cellulose sponges disintegrate rapidly leaving bits in the clay which can cause problems later. A **pin tool** is needed to evenly trim thrown rims. To trim away excess clay from the base of a thrown object, a wooden knife is best. Use a cutting wire of metal or nylon to cut the thrown piece from the wheelhead. A bowl containing thin slurry should be kept next to the wheel to use as a lubricant during throwing.

A **barrier cream** may be used to protect the hands from possible skin problems due to prolonged contact with water. This type of cream is applied before immersion, acting as a shield to prevent dry and cracked skin. One such cream is Kerodex 71 (Ayerst Laboratories) available at most pharmacies.

PREPARING TO THROW

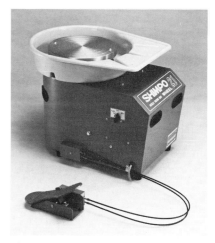

Shimpo electric wheel. Model RK-10.

AMACO Kickwheel No. 3-D.

The basic tools needed for throwing.

KNEADING

For best results on the wheel, properly kneaded clay is essential. First, weigh a ball of clay. This practice will assist in determining the finished size of a thrown piece. Then thoroughly knead the ball of clay. (See Chapter 2 for details on kneading procedure.) Correctly done, the clay will be completely homogenized and contain no air bubbles.

CENTERING

Sit comfortably and close to the wheel, with tools, slurry and clay within reach. Start the wheel turning slowly. The direction of the turn is important — most right-handed people find it best to have the wheel turning counterclockwise, while left-handed people prefer to turn the wheel clockwise. If the wheel is turning counterclockwise, place the right hand in the "top hand" position and the left hand in the "side hand" position. If the wheel is to be turned clockwise, simply reverse hand positions.

Drop a ball of clay, without mashing it out of shape, onto the slowly turning, dry wheelhead. Lubricate the hands and clay with a thin film of slurry. Bring the wheel up to top speed. The greater the speed, the less time and pressure are needed to bring the clay to center.

Position the side hand elbow against the hipbone so that the back muscles can give added pressure for centering. Lock the top hand arm firmly against the side of the body to use the shoulder muscles for downward pressure. In this position, the body does the work and the arms and wrists will not tire as easily.

To secure the clay to the wheel, slowly increase downward pressure with the top hand palm just behind the center of the clay ball. During this movement, rest the side hand against the side of the clay. When the ball is safely attached, increase pressure with the side hand to help center the clay. One hand should use more pressure than the other for each move. If both hands use the same force, the clay wobbles around and will not center. Quick motions or pressure changes will knock the clay off center. Lubricate the clay and hands sparingly by applying slurry with the sponge.

After the clay has been relatively centered, place the top hand directly opposite the side hand. Slowly squeeze the clay upward into a narrow cone with both palms. Several passes may be required to create a cone. Use slowly diminishing, even pressure or the top of the cone will be torn off. Next, use the top hand to slowly push the cone downward. A slight off-side pressure can help move the clay more easily while the side hand acts as a guide. Repeat these up and down movements several times to insure that the clay is truly centered.

A.

B.

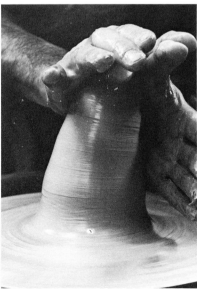

C.

A. Using downward pressure to secure the clay to the spinning wheel.

B. Squeezing the clay upward with both palms.

C. Pushing the cone downward.

OPENING UP THE CLAY

Once the ball of clay is completely centered, brace the arms against the body and place the palms opposite each other so that they rest lightly against the spinning clay. With thumb tips touching, push them downward into the center of the clay until they are about ¾ (1.9 cm) inch from the bottom. Do not raise the wrists or change hand positions, otherwise the clay will go out of center. If the thumbs do not reach down far enough, push the clay walls downward with the web between thumb and index finger of both hands. When the correct depth is reached, squeeze each thumb tip toward the palm to widen the opening and cup the palms under the ball to compact the clay at the base. Keep the arms firmly braced at the sides during the entire procedure.

An alternate method: With the arms braced at the sides, place all the fingers of the top hand over the center of the spinning ball, with the thumb against the side hand for leverage. Arch the fingers and push them into the clay to the proper depth. Then draw them toward the side hand to widen the hole.

Pushing a hole into the centered clay with both thumbs.

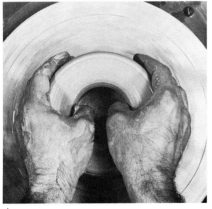

A.

D.

B.

C.

A. Opening the hole with the thumbs.

B. Cupping the base to compact the clay.

C. An alternate way to make the hole by using all the fingers of the top hand.

D. Opening the hole with the hand.

THROWING BASIC FORMS

CYLINDER

All wheel forms are variations of a cylinder. It is therefore important to learn to make this form correctly.

After the clay has been centered and the hole opened, it is necessary to change the position of the hands. Brace both arms against the sides of the body. With palms facing and fingers pointing straight down, put the side hand inside the hole and the top hand directly opposite on the outside. Lock the thumbs together for stability. The hands must be placed in this manner or the fingers will dig into the clay. In other words, right-handers work on the right side of the wheel and left-handers to the left.

With the hands at the bottom of the piece, slightly cup the fingers and squeeze the clay like a pincers. As the wheel spins rapidly, slowly begin to pull the clay upward. Move the outside hand up a bit until both hands are directly opposite, otherwise the clay will move outward rather than up. Slowly reduce the pressure near the top to leave a thicker rim.

Pulling up the wall with the tips of the fingers of both hands.

Another view of pulling up the wall.

Repeat these movements, starting at the bottom each time and reducing the pressure as the hands pull the clay up. Too much pressure will twist the cylinder or tear off the upper portion of the clay. Apply light lubrication with the sponge as needed. Resist the temptation to apply lots of water to keep the clay running smoothly through the hands. Water is rapidly absorbed which will cause the clay to become too soft and collapse.

As the cylinder grows taller, run the wheel more slowly. High centrifugal force can throw the top off center and cause collapse. If the walls of the cylinder are uneven or large spirals begin to form in the walls, the ratio of wheel speed to upward hand motion must be adjusted. The slower the wheel turns, the slower the hands must move.

To prevent the cylinder from growing wider at the top, be sure that the forearms stay braced against the sides while the elbows slide slowly to the rear. If the elbows stay locked against the sides of the body, the hands swing outward in an arc, moving the clay with them.

Use the pin tool to correct an uneven lip. Lock the arms against the body and hold the pin tool with the outside hand. Leave enough of the pin free to pass through the clay wall. Aim the pin in the same direction the wheel is turning. Slowly ease the pin through the cylinder wall until the point touches a finger of the inside hand, then quickly lift upward. This gives a smooth, level lip which can be thickened or rounded with the sponge. A piece of leather might be used instead of a sponge for a more finished look.

Using a pin tool to trim the top of a cylinder.

Finishing the rim with a piece of leather.

Cutting From the Wheel

Hold the wooden knife like a pencil with the outside hand. Use firm support from the other hand. To remove excess clay, make an angled cut into the base of the moderately spinning piece. Then make a flat cut underneath the waste clay to free it from the wheel. Stop the wheel and remove the cut clay.

To cut the finished piece free, take the cutting wire firmly, one end in each hand, and draw it taut. Turn the wheel slowly and pull the wire under the cylinder from the back, across the wheelhead toward the body.

Lift the piece from the stopped wheel by grasping its base with the wide open first and second fingers of each hand. Turn the wheel slightly to break the friction. **Pot lifters** can also be used to take a piece from the wheel.

The entire foregoing process should be practiced again and again until a natural rhythm occurs between wheel, clay and artist.

Cutting excess clay from the base with a wooden knife.

Releasing the cylinder from the wheel by pulling a taut wire under the slowly turning clay.

Removing the cylinder from the wheel.

BATS

If large diameter cylinders are needed, it is best to throw them on a bat. Bats can be made from wood, plastic, or any stiff material. However, plaster bats are most useful. The plaster absorbs water and aids in drying the finished piece. (See Chapter 10 for information on how to make bats.)

Apply a thin coat of slurry to the wheelhead and the bottom of the bat. With a slight twisting motion, press the bat onto the wheelhead

Peeling away the cut clay.

until it is stuck tightly. Dampen the top of the bat, center and throw the clay as usual.

To remove the finished work from the wheelhead, slide a wide knife, metal scraper, or spatula under the slowly turning bat until it is free. Stop the wheel and set the finished piece aside. When it has stiffened, the clay should simply come away from the bat with no cutting needed.

THROWING A BOWL

A bowl form is simply a short, wide, curved cylinder. Therefore all of the procedures necessary in making a cylinder apply, starting with properly kneaded clay and centering. Open the hole to the approximate width of the base desired and pull up the wall. To put the desired curve into the wall, use the **stretching method.** With the wheel turning at moderate speed, set one finger of the outside hand lightly against the side of the rim. Slowly raise the fingers of the inside hand, pushing the clay outward. After several light passes, the wall should be complete. Level the rim with the pin tool if necessary and finish with a sponge or piece of leather.

Do not stretch the clay too far or the piece will collapse. If stretch marks appear, use the outside hand to push the wall inward slightly while the inside hand controls the rim. For larger forms, grasp a **rib** of metal, wood, or rubber with the inside hand to more easily stretch the wall.

Throw wide or large bowls on a bat. Remember that the wider the bowl, the faster the rim is spinning — too fast and centrifugal force will cause the form to collapse.

TRIMMING

For most applications, trimming can be easily accomplished by carving away excess clay with a knife. If a more finished look is desired, trimming should be done in the following manner.

Many different shapes and styles of trimming tools are commercially available. Tools can also be made from spring steel, old band saw blades or any flat metal that can be given a sharp edge. Round wire sculpture tools are not very good for trimming purposes. Tools must be kept sharp for best results.

Allow the thrown piece to dry slowly until it is stiff enough to be turned upside down and placed on the wheel. Before inverting the

Curving the wall by stretching the clay from inside.

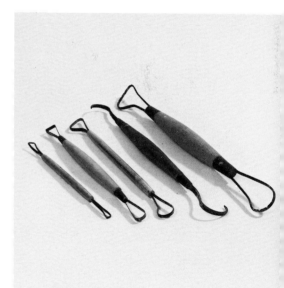
An assortment of trimming tools.

piece, check the wall thickness to estimate the amount of trimming needed. Center the object by holding a finger near its side while slowly turning the wheel. If the finger touches in one place, stop the wheel and slightly move the piece directly opposite to that position. Continue to check in this manner until the work is in center. Secure the work to the wheel with several small pats of clay evenly spaced around the rim.

Brace the outside hand arm against the leg or side of the body. Hold the trimming tool with the cutting edge at a 45° angle to the clay surface. Brace the inside hand arm against the leg or side and press the thumb against the other hand for greater support. Rest the middle finger of the inside hand on the center of the piece to help prevent it from accidentally flying off the wheel.

Bring the wheel up to throwing speed and carefully begin to cut away unwanted clay. If the clay is the proper consistency, long strips of clay will seemingly leap off the surface. If the tool sticks in the clay, remove the work and allow it more time to stiffen. If short bits of clay come off the piece, it is too stiff to easily trim. Sometimes it is possible to wet the clay again and then trim it.

Trimming marks are often very noticeable, particularly in grogged clay. To make such marks less obvious, throw over them with a rounded wooden tool pressing in any exposed grog.

Trimming the base of a spinning cylinder.

Joining wheel-thrown parts is accomplished in the same way that coils or slab forms are put together. After the parts have been thrown, trimmed and allowed to stiffen, score the areas to be joined with a toothed scraper or piece of hacksaw blade. Apply vinegar to each piece and firmly press the parts together. Use a modeling tool to work clay from each piece into the joint. Add a small coil of clay to fill and smooth the seam if necessary.

As with other sculptural forms, it is a good idea to sketch a wheel-thrown sculpture in advance. Note all dimensions and where any joining is to be done. Throw all the parts, trim them and allow them to stiffen sufficiently before attempting assembly. It is important to drill holes in all parts of the form so that steam can escape during firing. If the sculpture has any hollow parts that are completely enclosed, they will explode.

JOINING PARTS

A sculpture made predominantly of assembled wheel-thrown parts.
Professor Turker Ozdogan, *Flugel Hornist*, 1985. Salt sprayed, reduction-fired stoneware, 54 x 19″ (137.2 x 48.1 cm).

Patricia Uchill Simons, *Blood Hound*.
Glazed stoneware,
18 x 14 x 12″ (45.7 x 35.6 x 30.1 cm).
Photograph: Chee Heng Yeong.

Right:
Author, *Knight*.
Glazed stoneware, velvet,
30″ (76.2 cm) tall.
Collection: Donald and Mary Melville.

Author, *HippoPOTamus*.
Glazed stoneware,
9 x 16 x 7″ (22.9 x 40.6 x 17.8 cm).
Collection: Nathan and Anita Sloane.

Some sculptures cannot be completely assembled before firing because of the weight of the clay parts or the design of the form. In such cases, provisions must be made in advance so that the pieces can be secured to each other after firing. Works could be designed with built-in flanges and sleeves to fit together like pipes. Certain forms might have holes strategically drilled so that they could be pinned together later with wooden dowels or metal rods. Others may be attached with glue or cement.

Wheel-thrown sculpture assembled after firing. Steffanie Samuels, *Rusted Spades*. Glazed stoneware, 60 x 23 x 23″ (152.4 x 58.4 x 58.4 cm). Photograph: R.H. Hensleigh.

Somewhere near the center of the ceramic art/craft spectrum sits a large group of forms identified by the awkward appellation: sculptural vessels. These objects seem to be categorized as neither utilitarian containers nor full-fledged "Fine Art" sculpture.

The vast majority of these works come from sculptors who have worked their way through the pottery studio, learning the tools and tricks of the trade. After making hundreds of pots — usually high quality pieces steeped in tradition — these clayworkers become tired of replicating ancient forms and yearn to break new visual ground without forsaking their familiar medium. Thus a particular difficulty arises. The clayworker who has been thoroughly schooled in the intricacies of the clay medium has usually accomplished this at the expense of developing a sense of the complexities of sculpture. While the two are not mutually exclusive, time has often been the major factor.

SCULPTURAL VESSELS

A thrown and slab constructed sculptural vessel.
Jerry Rothman, *Ritual Vessel*, 1985. Glazed mid-range porcelain, 16" (40.6 cm) tall.

Left:
Altered thrown and coil-built sculptural vessel.
Chris Gustin, *Ewer*, 1988. Reduction-fired glazed stoneware, 16 x 11 x 7" (41 x 28 x 18 cm).
Photograph: Andrew Dean Powell.

Right:
Pre-Columbian sculptural vessel from Costa Rica. *Alligator Pot.* Earthenware, 9⅜ x 6¼ x 8" (23.8 x 15.9 x 20.3 cm).
Worcester Art Museum.
Bequest of Charles B. Cohn, in memory of Stuart P. Anderson.

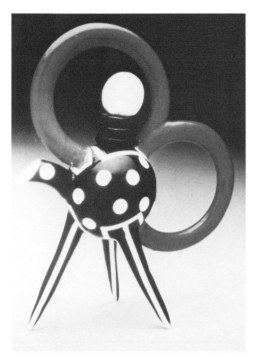

Slipcast and assembled sculptural vessel.
Riki Moss, *Memphis Spot Series*.
Glazed lowfire clay, underglazes, china paint,
19″ (48.3 cm) tall.
Photograph: Ralph Gabriner.

A second problem plagues some of these artists. In their desire to shake off a perceived second class status and seek "legitimacy" in the world of Fine Art, the work presented fails to compete in any realm.

Today, many ceramic works do not necessarily fit the prevailing definitions of either Fine Art sculpture or usable containers. To understand these objects better, one might use the principles of design and composition discussed in Chapter 1 as a basis for discovery. Discard the psychological and sociological baggage, then examine and appreciate each piece individually as an expression of humanity in three-dimensional form.

A slab-built sculptural vessel.
Elyse Saperstein, *Roller Teapot*.
Terra-cotta, slips, terra sigillata,
11 x 8 x 4″ (27.9 x 20.3 x 10.2 cm).
Photograph: John Carlano.

Five-part thrown and carved sculptural vessel.
Nancy Frommer LaPointe, *Twin Jars #1*.
Terra-cotta, slips, pewter patina,
3 x 3 x 7″ (7.6 x 7.6 x 17.8 cm).
Photograph: Michael Cohen.

Thrown plates used as part of a
sculptural wall panel.
Thomas Maltbie, *Wall Piece*, 1987.
Clay, wood, paper, bamboo, 37 x
69 x 4″ (94 x 175.3 x 10.2 cm).
Photograph: Ron Forth.

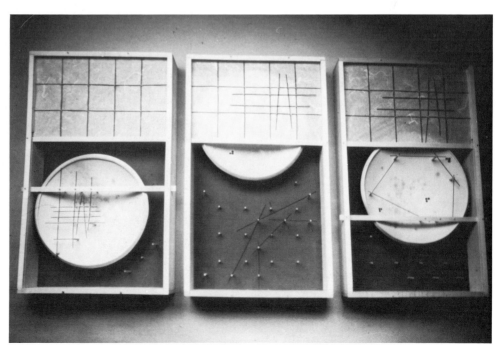

7 SURFACE TREATMENT

A smooth surface provides the tranquil setting
for an intimate encounter.
Kathryn Besley, *Issy*, 1985.
Matt-glazed porcelain,
10 x 9½ x 6½" (25.4 x 24.1 x 16.5 cm).
Photograph: Allan Laughmiller.

Burnishing the clay surface can give a high
sheen to lowfired sculpture.
Roberta Griffith, *Dōtaku Totem*, 1989.
Burnished whiteware, sawdust fired,
20½ x 13½ x 6" (52.1 x 34.3 x 15.2 cm).
Photograph: John Willis.

There are several techniques that give a sculpture a finished look before glazing and firing. Often, the most effective surface enhancement comes from the technique used to create the sculpture: modeling or carving tool marks, impressions left from pinch forming or coil lines. Sometimes, a totally plain surface may enhance a finished work. In this case, the surface merely needs to be smoothed. More often however, varied or enriched surfaces can bring greater impact.

Whatever the effect desired, there are several specific times during the evolution of a clay sculpture when the surface can be easily developed: while the clay is still plastic, when it has reached the leather-hard stage and after it has dried.

AT WHAT STAGE?

SMOOTHING THE CLAY

If a sculpture with a smooth surface is desired, this may be accomplished during any of the development stages. Trying to smooth the surface after the clay has dried completely, however, can often result in the opposite effect. Therefore, smoothing during the first two stages is advisable.

While the object is under construction, draw a flat wooden rib or hard rubber kidney rib over the exterior until it is uniform. Flatten any problem areas by lightly beating them with a smooth wooden paddle.

When the clay has reached the leather-hard stage, use flexible metal ribs to further even out the clay. At this point the clay can be brought to a highly polished finish by **burnishing.** With a circular motion, rub a spoon or other rounded object over the outside of the sculpture. Rub only one small area at a time until the area has been polished. This process should be repeated two or three times. Apply a thin coating of vegetable oil between rubbings to help control drying. Burnishing is most effective on works that are fired to low temperatures. Objects fired above cone 06 (991° C/1816° F) lose their shine.

After the clay has dried, attempts to further refine the clay can often reverse the process. Working the dry surface with a damp sponge will lift off a fine layer of clay and expose any grog or coarse clay particles, making the surface rough. Attempting to smooth the dry clay with sandpaper will usually do the same thing. Sanding can clog the pores of the clay with dust and impede any glazing. If smoothing the surface at this stage is necessary, sand the surface being sure to remove all particles by carefully vacuuming or blowing. Do not use a damp sponge as this only clogs the pores. The textures that result from these activities can often be pleasing in their own right.

WHEN CLAY IS PLASTIC

Several imaginative textures can be introduced while the clay is still soft. Compose areas of relief decoration by **pressing** the clay from the inside or **pinching** from the outside. To prevent the piece from deforming, support the clay wall from the opposite side when using either of these methods.

Introduce repeat motifs by **stamping** the surface with found objects such as bits of wood, small stones, nuts and bolts or any small items. Remember to support the clay wall from behind while stamping to prevent distortion. Stamps with specific designs can be modeled in clay and then fired or carved in plaster. Be sure that the decoration developed has no undercuts, otherwise it will pull on the clay and not print well.

Small bits, patches, balls or a thick paste of clay can be **modeled-on** or **appliquéd** to the damp clay form to produce texture in certain areas or over the entire surface.

Use a piece of sawblade, a toothed scraper, comb, or any serrated edge to **scratch** a decoration into the clay.

Scratching creates an active surface on this work.
Nancy Frommer LaPointe, *Long Boat #4*.
Terra-cotta, slips, 16 x 13 x 24″ (40.6 x 33 x 61 cm).
Photograph: Michael Cohen.

A thick paste of clay is used to create an active surface.
Rosette Gault, *Ceremonial Vase*, 1988.
Glazed earthenware, 14 x 10 x 3½" (35.6 x 25.4 x 8.9 cm).

Garden sculpture embellished with stamped decoration.
Zeljko Kujundzic, *The Prince*.
Unglazed earthenware, 30" (76.2 cm) tall.

A sculpture with highlighted incised surface.
Harris Deller, *Untitled Teapot With Lines,
Cross-Hatching and Passive Spout*, 1988.
Reduction-fired porcelain, inlaid black glaze,
16 x 11 x 4½" (40.6 x 27.9 x 11.4 cm).
Photograph: Duane Powell.

WHEN CLAY IS LEATHER-HARD

Use sharp modeling or carving tools, knives or dental instruments to
incise, or carve in, ornamental configurations when the clay has
reached the leather-hard stage. The reverse of this process is called **excising:** Cutting away the background to expose a raised relief.

Piercing, or cutting through the form, is also best done at this stage
of drying.

Piercing a form creates a sense of expanded
volume. Zeljko Kujundzic, *Ancestor.*
Glazed stoneware, 22" (55.9 cm) tall.

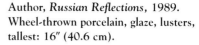
Author, *Russian Reflections*, 1989.
Wheel-thrown porcelain, glaze, lusters,
tallest: 16″ (40.6 cm).

Juanita M. Moody, *Dumped On*.
Handbuilt, press molded stoneware, colored slips,
7 x 18 x 45″ (17.8 x 45.7 x 114.3 cm).

Patriciu Mateescu,
Jetta,
1988. Slipcast,
lowfire clay, glaze, 4
feet (1.2 m) tall.
Photograph: the
artist.

COLOR 1

Dora De Larios, *The World According to Dora.*
Slab-built porcelain, glazes, gold leaf, 7½ x 40'
(2.3 x 12.2 m).
Location: Hilton Hotel, Anaheim, California.
Photograph: Tad Bonsall.

Alison Palmer, *Cow Girl.*
Handbuilt whiteware, underglazes, glaze,
36 x 38 x 14" (91.4 x 96.5 x 35.6 cm).
Photograph: Gary Kessler.

COLOR 2

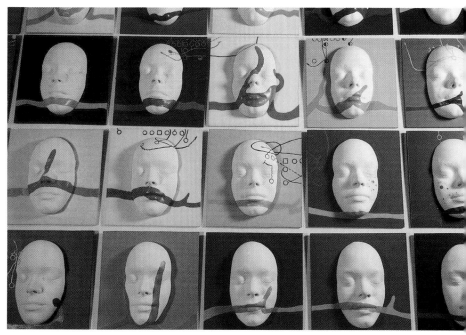

Helena M. Oberg, *Laughter and Forgetting (April '85)* (detail).
Press-molded life mask, whiteware, wood, paint.
11 x 4′ (3.4 x 1.2 m).
Photograph: the author.

Jack Thompson (AKA Jugo de Vegetales).
Vida Eterna, 1985.
Press-molded, modeled whiteware, acrylic paint,
65 x 16 x 22″ (165.1 x 40.6 x 55.9 cm).

Josephine Gerrard, *Jane*.
Handbuilt earthenware, plaster, terra sigillata,
acrylic paint,
26 x 32 x 13″ (66 x 81.3 x 33 cm).
Photograph: Steve Selvin.

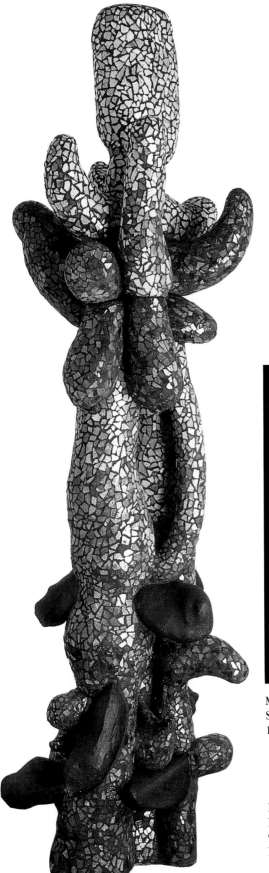

Louis Vaccaro, *Teapots (decorative)*.
Slab-built whiteware, airbrushed underglazes,
largest: 10 x 8 x 2½″ (25.4 x 20.3 x 6.4 cm).

Marcia Polenberg, *Construction*.
Slipcast slab whiteware, glaze, paint,
13½ x 14″ (34.3 x 35.6 cm).

Roy Cartwright, *Flower #3*, 1989.
Press-molded, coil-built earthenware, glazed tile mosaic.
92″ (233.7 cm) tall.
Photograph: Jay Bachemin.

Dennis Peak, *Rhapsody*, 1988.
Handbuilt whiteware, underglazes, matt glaze,
30 x 90 x 4″ (76.2 x 228.6 x 10.2 cm).

Thomas W. Lollar, *Ritz Tower*.
Slab-built, mid-range stoneware, luster, paint,
62 x 16 x 16″ (157.5 x 40.6 x 40.6 cm).

Mona Adisa Brooks, *Safe Trip*.
Handbuilt porcelain, glaze stains, oxides, luster,
10 x 10 x 10″ (25.4 x 25.4 x 25.4 cm).
Photograph: Bobby Hansson.

Susan Risi, *Love Birds*.
Extruded stoneware, oxides, glaze stains,
40 x 26 x 15″ (101.6 x 66 x 38.1 cm).

Nancy Jurs, *Chryseis*, 1987.
Handbuilt stoneware, acrylic paint,
34 x 18 x 10″ (86.4 x 45.7 x 25.4 cm).

Riki Moss, *Teapot*.
Slipcast, assembled whiteware, underglazes, glazes,
china paints,
12″ (30.5 cm) tall.
Photograph: Ralph Gabriner.

Dennis Clive, *Big Day at the Races (Bugatti Type 35)*, 1987.
Handbuilt whiteware, underglazes, glaze, china paint, luster,
21 x 60 x 30″ (53.3 x 152.4 x 76.2 cm).
Photograph: DC Works.

Toby Buonagurio, *Flaming Mane Robot*, 1988.
Handbuilt whiteware, glazes, lusters, acrylic paint, glitter,
28 x 14½ x 13½″ (71.1 x 36.8 x 34.3 cm).
Photograph: Edgar Buonagurio.

Sylvia Hyman, *Sporophore Series "Swan Award"*, 1982.
Slab-built stoneware and porcelain,
17½″ (44 cm) tall.
Collection: Duncan Phillips.
Photograph: Larry Dixon.

Margaret Keelan, *Naomi in White Dress, Seated*, 1988.
Handbuilt porcelain, oil paint,
34 x 15 x 12″ (61 x 38.1 x 30.5 cm).
Photograph: Richard Sargent.

AFTER CLAY IS DRY

When the clay form has completely dried only minor surface changes can be accomplished. **Scraping** with serrated tools can alter the surface slightly.

Use a sharp implement to **sgraffito,** or draw delicate lines, into the dry clay. This method works best on fine-grained clays. Precise definition can be lost on coarse or heavily-grogged clay bodies.

Sgraffito on this work enlivens part of the surface and creates contrast.
Floyd Gompf, *Shield.*
Raku fired clay, underglaze, concrete, steel wire, 48 x 48 x 12" (121.9 x 121.9 x 30.5 cm).
Photograph: Joe Z.

Two different scraped textures offer a lively surface contrast.
Robert L. Glover, *Trinitas.*
Earthenware,
43 x 36 x 3" (109.2 x 91.4 x 7.6 cm).
Photograph: Susan Einstein.

8 FINISHES

Dark slip applied to wet clay creates a lively contrasting surface decoration.
Ann Christenson, *Untitled,* 1985.
Unglazed porcelain, slip, steel,
43 x 22 x 15″ (109.2 x 55.9 x 38.1 cm).
Photograph: Ben Blackwell.

COLOR

The wide array of rich natural color that can emerge from fired clay is often the only touch needed to finish a work of ceramic sculpture. Depending upon the type of clay used, the firing temperature and atmosphere in the kiln, colors can range from white through sand, buff and brick red, to tan, brown, chocolate and black, with virtually endless variations in between.

Sometimes, however, these colors need to be intensified, altered, augmented, or even obliterated. These changes or additions, like surface treatments in Chapter 7, can be done at different stages of the sculpture's development.

LEATHER-HARD

When the object is in the leather-hard stage of drying, colored **washes, slips** or **engobes** can be applied. A wash is a small amount of coloring oxide, such as copper carbonate or iron oxide, thoroughly mixed with water. A slip is a slurry of the same clay to which colorant has been added. An engobe is composed of certain glaze compounds combined to make a colored clay-like slurry.

Each of these materials can be thinly brushed, poured, dipped or sprayed onto the damp surface of a sculpture to enhance or contrast with the natural color of the clay. If the decoration is applied too thickly it can appear artificial, detract from the form of the work or crack off when it dries. However, carefully built-up layers of different colored slips can sometimes create a decorative low-relief effect. This technique is known as **pâte-sur-pâte.**

After these coloring agents have been applied, allow the object to dry then bisque fire it. Next, apply a clear or translucent glaze to the work and fire it to the maturing temperature of the glaze. (Note: While ceramic tradition calls for the work to be fired to the maturing temperature of the clay to insure its proper **vitrification** — making it waterproof — this is not necessarily a prerequisite for sculpture. A poorly fired or underfired glaze, however, can destroy the desired visual effects. For best results, the work should be fired to the recommended glaze temperature.)

When the high shine of a glazed surface is not desired, the decorated piece can be left unglazed and fired slowly to maturity. The resulting finish will usually be dry matt and the underglaze colors will be fairly flat in tone. The oxide washes will generally take on a dark metallic quality.

This surface is a variation of pâte-sur-pâte using thick slip with lumps of dry clay mixed in. Gail Caulfield, *City Dog,* 1988 (detail). Glazed whiteware, body stains, 58 x 27 x 34" (147.3 x 68.6 x 86.4 cm) Photograph: the artist.

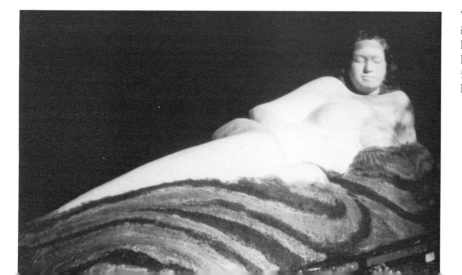

These colors are derived from oxides wedged into clay and applied over the form. Lorraine Capparell, *Sleeping Butte III,* 1985. Reduction fired terra-cotta, oxides, 57 x 20 x 23" (144.8 x 50.8 x 58.4 cm). Photograph: the artist/Lars Speyer.

Brilliant brushed underglazes suggest
movement in this sculpture.
Judy M. Hiramoto. *Feud*, © 1988.
Glazed whiteware, underglazes,
15 x 11 x 9" (38.1 x 27.9 x 23.9 cm).
Photograph: the artist.

Airbrushed and pen-drawn underglazes produce
the illusion of depth in this wall piece.
Daisy Brand, *Interiors*.
Unglazed porcelain, underglazes, wood,
26 x 22 x 4" (66 x 55.9 x 10.2 cm).
Photograph: Hillel Burger.

DRY

Colored washes and engobes can be applied to dry clay with the same methods used for leather-hard clay. It is necessary to thin them before use in order to prevent undue buildup and to avoid peeling as they dry.

Commercial **underglazes** provide an almost infinite variety of colors which can be applied to dry clay. Underglaze is available in several different forms: dry powder, which must be mixed with certain oils; semi-moist cakes, to be mixed with water; water-soluble pastes, pre-mixed in tubes; and pre-mixed liquids in jars. Each type of underglaze can be applied easily by brushing or spraying. Although underglaze can be poured or dipped, so much of it would be needed, these methods are usually impractical.

To draw line decorations on dry clay, use commercial **underglaze crayon.**

Underglazes will fire with a pastel-like hue and a flat or velvety finish. Clear or translucent glazes must be fired over them to bring out their more brilliant hues.

BISQUE

Engobes, washes, and underglazes can also be applied to bisque fired objects. **Underglaze pencil** works better on bisqued clay than on dry because it will not dig into the surface. To intensify the colors, apply a clear or translucent glaze over the decorated work and fire to the maturing temperature of the glaze.

As noted earlier, ceramic tradition calls for firing clay objects to their maturity. In the case of sculpture, however, a simple hardening fire is sometimes all that is required. If this is the case, there are several nonfired finishes that can be employed.

Stains, or bisque stains, are either water- or oil-based. They are commercially available in myriad colors, densities and finishes. Brush or spray only one coat of a stain onto bisque fired ware, then let it dry. For certain effects such as "antiquing," lightly rub off the excess after the stain has been applied, leaving stain only in the recesses of the clay surface. When the first stain has dried, the same process can be used with other colors to create a patina effect. This is most effective when translucent stains are applied over opaques.

When dry, most stains have a soft matt look. They can be buffed with a cloth to obtain a satin sheen. After stains have dried, they are generally impervious to water and will resist fading. Some manufacturers claim that their product is permanent and can be used outdoors. Others suggest the use of certain sealers to provide wear resistance. Before embarking on an ambitious project, prudent testing is recommended. As a bonus, some bisque stains can be used on other materials as well such as wood, plaster, fabric, or paper.

Other nonfired coatings can be used effectively on bisque fired forms. To enhance the natural color of the clay, rub oils, waxes or even shoe polish into the clay. Then buff the surface to a soft sheen.

For startling novelty effects, **glitter** or **flocking** can be adhered to fired clay. Coat the clay evenly with slightly thinned white glue. Next, sprinkle a generous amount of the material onto the wet glue. When the glue has dried completely, blow or tap off any excess material. Be sure to apply the coatings evenly, otherwise bare patches might appear. Adding more glitter is fairly easy, but flocking is not.

Oil paint, acrylic and enamel paint can be brushed or sprayed onto bisque fired clay. Watercolor paint and dye can also be used, but coat them with clear varnish or acrylic to preserve their color.

A bisque stain was applied after firing for a patina effect. Rex Hendershot, *Centurion*. Unglazed terra-cotta, oil stain, 21″ (53.3 cm) tall. Dallas, TX.

A fantasy work glistening with glitter and flocking. Toby Buonagurio, *Tiger Sorceress*, 1985. Glazed whiteware, lusters, acrylic paint, glitter, flocking, 23 x 21 x 18½″ (58.4 x 53.3 x 47 cm). Photograph: Edgar Buonagurio.

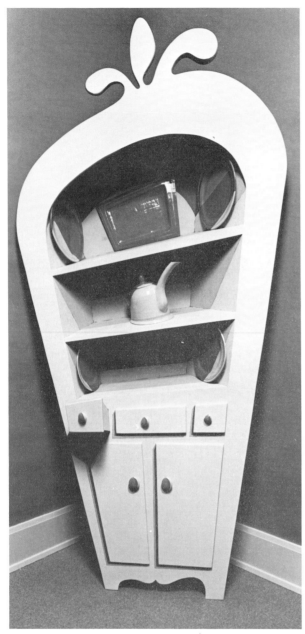

Mixed media sculpture colored with acrylic paints.
Ron Dale, *Corner Cupboard*, 1984.
Whiteware, wood, acrylic paint,
11 x 5 x 1½' (3.4 x 1.5 x .5 m).
Photograph: William Martin.

Underglaze pencil provides the delicate line drawings
in this wall work.
Paula Winokur, *Site X: Mesa Memory*, 1987.
Reduction fired unglazed porcelain, metallic sulfates,
ceramic pencil, 47 x 21 x 11″ (119.4 x 53.3 x 27.9 cm).
Courtesy: Helen Drutt Gallery, New York and
Philadelphia. Photograph: © Eric Mitchell.

The most exciting, eye-catching manner by which to emphasize the intrinsic qualities of clay sculpture is through the use of glaze. It is also probably the most complicated and confusing aspect of working in ceramics.

Even if glaze is applied to a piece directly from a jar that has the right numbers, it will still be helpful to have a basic understanding of what glazes are, how they are made, and how to make them work. To this end, only that information deemed most useful to sculptors will be discussed. Highly technical information will not be considered in this text.

Glaze is a thin coating of a glass-like compound which, when fused to a ceramic surface by heat, provides a protective coating against weathering and discoloration, gives additional strength and makes the object relatively impervious to liquids and acids. Glaze also helps a piece look nice.

Glazes may be transparent, translucent or opaque. They come in a wide range of finishes from high gloss to matt as well as highly textured surfaces.

Different glazes have different maturing points — the temperature at which their ingredients have reached complete fusion. It is this aspect that is most necessary to understand before working with glazes, either studio prepared or from a jar. The choice of glaze depends, to a great extent upon the clay being used. For best results, use a glaze that has the same firing range as the clay. This will help prevent many disappointments (referred to by many as "flaws") after the piece has been fired. In some cases, glazes that have a lower maturing temperature than the clay can also be used.

GLAZE TYPES

There are many types of glazes that are used extensively in the realm of pottery. While any of these could be employed more or less successfully with clay sculpture, the following selection will probably be most helpful. Always test a glaze on a sample piece before committing it to a major work.

Gloss Glaze
The most prevalent of glaze types at all firing temperatures, gloss glaze has a smooth, hard, shiny surface when properly fired. Gloss glazes intensify the colors of most underglazes. They also exude the brightest hues when colorants are mixed into them. The major drawback to us-

GLAZES

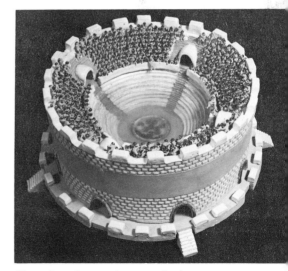

Clear gloss glaze used over underglazes to intensify their colors.
Douglas Baldwin, *Flood*.
Glazed earthenware, underglazes,
7 x 15 x 15" (17.8 x 38.1 x 38.1 cm).

Matt glaze softens underglaze colors in this sculpture by Judy M. Hiramoto. *Desert,* © 1985. Glazed whiteware, underglazes, 16 x 24 x 9″ (40.6 x 60.1 x 22.9 cm). Photograph: the artist.

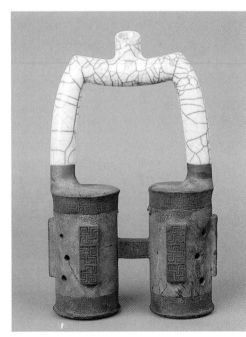

Crackle glaze accentuates the mouthpiece on this tuned ceremonial vessel flute. Robin L. Hodgkinson, *Maya Jazz.* Raku fired whiteware, oxide washes, engobe, 12 x 6 x 2″ (30.5 x 15.2 x 5.1 cm).

ing them on complex sculptural works is that they are highly reflective which can obscure many subtleties of the form. Another problem with gloss glazes is that they tend to run if overfired.

Slip Glaze

Many common earthenware clays, when fired above cone 8 (1236° C/ 2257° F), melt to form a glossy, brownish glaze. To aid in the melting, add a small amount of **frit** or **feldspar.** Ten percent is usually all that is needed. A slip glaze works best when applied to leather-hard clay. If the slip and clay dry evenly, there is less chance that the glaze will crawl or run off during the fire. While this type of glaze is certainly easy enough to make and can have fascinating variations in color and surface, the high shine may camouflage nuances of the sculptural form.

Matt Glaze

A true matt glaze is one that is fully matured and smooth but has no shine. Good matt glazes may have a satin sheen or a "buttery" quality. They will conceal most underglaze decoration. Colorants added to the glaze tend to give softer, more pastel shades. Properly fired matt glazes rarely shift or run. A minor inconvenience may be that, because of its crystalline surface structure, a matt glaze could be hard to keep clean.

Crackle Glaze

A crackle glaze is one that has been made deliberately to **craze,** creating a web of cracks throughout the glaze. Usually considered a flaw, controlled crazing can be an effective decoration. To accent the fired crackle pattern, brush strong tea or waterproof inks over the surface and rub off the excess. The color stays in the cracks leaving a network of dark lines in contrast to the glaze. To make the effect more permanent, rub in coloring oxides instead of ink. Then refire the work to a slightly higher temperature. This will mature the glaze and leave the crackle pattern intact.

Commercial Glazes

The permutations and combinations in the world of commercial glaze possibilities boggles the mind. Although none of the purported effects are guaranteed by their manufacturers (read the labels), most of the glazes work most of the time. They are relatively expensive compared to studio-mixed glazes, but the time and necessary experimentation saved may be worth the expense. Be sure to rigorously test any glaze before using it on an important work.

Now that the important decisions regarding the type of glaze, color and temperature have been made, it is necessary to get the glaze properly onto the bisque fired work so that it will provide adequate coverage, produce the desired results when fired, and not run off the piece or otherwise detract from the final result.

PREPARATION

Before applying any glaze, be sure that the object is free of dust, dirt and hand oils. **Protect the eyes with goggles or a face shield** and blow off any dust or dirt. Wiping with a sponge or cloth will only clog the pores of the bisqued clay and prevent proper glaze adhesion. Wash oily pieces with soap, rinse and let dry thoroughly before applying glaze.

If a work is to be only partially glazed, cover unglazed areas with **wax resist.** Brush on a thin coating of wax. This will prevent the glaze from being absorbed into the clay. Before firing, sponge off any glaze that has clung to the wax. If wax accidentally gets onto portions of the work that are to be glazed, scrape off as much as possible. Melt away the rest with judicious use of a lighted match. Do not concentrate the heat in one area for too long or the sculpture might crack. If a great mistake has been made, place the work into a kiln and slowly heat the entire piece to about 200° C (392° F). This will volatilize all the wax. When the piece has completely cooled, reapply the wax resist properly.

Unglazed areas may also be blocked off with masking tape. Be sure to stick all the leading edges firmly to the clay. Otherwise glaze will seep underneath the tape and spoil the desired effect. Remove the tape before firing to prevent ash from accidentally spoiling the glaze.

Remember that to prevent a sculpture from fusing to a kiln shelf during firing, the bottom of the form should not be glazed. Protect this area with wax resist or masking tape.

INTERIORS

It is a good idea to glaze the inside of a ceramic sculpture, if possible, even if the interior of a hollow ceramic sculpture is not going to be visible in its final pose. Applying a glaze too thickly or unevenly only on the outside can cause fracturing. During the firing, tension and compression strains develop in the clay body. If too much tension builds up in an area because of glaze thickness, the clay will split at its thinnest point. Equal glazing inside and out will help prevent such breaks.

GLAZING

Colorful combinations of commercial glazes dance around this work.
Riki Moss, *Untitled.*
Glazed slipcast whiteware, underglaze,
16″ (40.6 cm) tall.
Photograph: Ralph Gabriner.

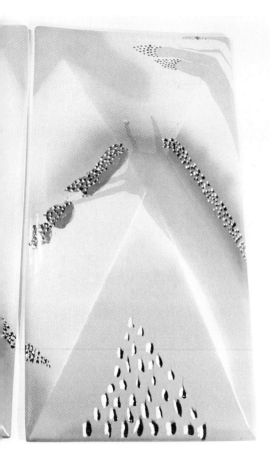

Poured glaze can also be used in a decorative manner, as shown on this large wall panel. Barbara J. Tiso, *Red Waterfall*, 1988 (right detail). Glazed slipcast whiteware, 25 x 53 x 5" (63.5 x 134.6 x 12.7 cm). Photograph: the artist.

POURING

The easiest way to glaze the outside of a ceramic form is to pour glaze over it. Place the object on a support in a container large enough in diameter to catch the excess glaze as it runs from the piece. Next, fill a pitcher with glaze and pour over the entire work as evenly as possible several times.

If the object and container are of reasonable size and weight, place them first on a bench wheel. By rotating the wheel while pouring, an even glaze thickness can be attained.

BRUSHING

The most common method of applying glaze to a sculpture is by brushing. It can also be the most time consuming. Brushing affords the most control and allows several colors to be applied in different areas of the work with little fear of overlapping. Large amounts of glaze are not necessary.

Always use good quality brushes. Because of their ability to hold large amounts of glaze, Japanese goat hair or hare's fur brushes are best suited to glazing. Most natural long bristle brushes are also acceptable. Nylon or other artificial bristle brushes do not hold as much glaze and can scrape off previous glaze coatings.

For an even application, thin the glaze slightly and brush on two or three coats. Load the brush well by fully dipping the bristles into the

Several glaze colors have been brushed on this wall piece. Mary Lou Alberetti, *Todi*. Glazed whiteware, underglazes, 17 x 20 x 1" (43.2 x 50.8 x 2.5 cm). Photograph: Jim Cordes.

glaze with a stirring motion. This action also helps prevent the glaze from settling in the container. Brush on the first coat with a light stroke. Immediately after the shine disappears, apply the next coat, drawing the strokes in the opposite direction. Crisscrossing the strokes will help fill in spots and low places, giving an evenly fired glaze.

SPRAYING

Spraying a glaze will produce the most even coating and preserve textural surfaces as well. **Proper safeguards are essential when spraying. Work in a spray booth with a good exhaust fan and exterior ventilating filter system. Use a quality air compressor with a medium duty spray gun capable of at least 25 psi (pounds per square inch) pressure. Wear a NIOSH approved respirator to prevent inhaling the dry powder — a paper mask is not sufficient. Wear plastic safety goggles to protect the eyes from airborne particles. If the object is too large for a spray booth, the next best option is to spray outdoors.**

Set the sculpture on a bench wheel in the spray booth. Sieve the glaze through a 60-mesh screen with enough water to obtain a smooth consistency of light cream. Fill the spray gun and hold it 16 to 18 inches (41 to 46 cm) from the form. Spray with a slow sweeping movement while slowly revolving the wheel. If the gun is too close to the object, the glaze will build-up and drip. Keep moving the gun and the sculpture to prevent uneven glazing. Spray from above and below to insure even glazing. Continue to spray until a fuzzy surface is built-up all over. Allow the glaze to dry completely before any cleanup is attempted. When dry, the glaze surface is quite powdery and must be handled as little as possible to prevent smudging.

Although spraying can give the best glaze surface, a great deal of glaze is wasted during the process. This can be collected periodically, test fired and possibly reconstituted for glazing.

DIPPING

Dipping is the quickest and easiest way to completely glaze a ceramic object. Dunk the work into the glaze, count to five and take it out. When dry, touch up any finger marks. This works best for small pieces. Obviously, it is impractical for large works because it would require too much glaze in giant containers as well as winches or muscle power to lift and submerge the sculpture.

Spraying offers the smoothest surface for underglaze or glaze.
Lynn Rachel Goldstein, *Wave Form.*
Unglazed whiteware, underglaze,
12 x 12 x 5″ (30.1 x 30.1 x 12.7 cm).
Photograph: Dean Powell.

With any of the aforementioned techniques, touch up can be done after the glaze has dried. Smooth lumps of glaze away by simply rubbing lightly with a finger. Fill in cracks or pinholes in the glaze by gently rubbing the glaze in a circular motion. Fill in chipped off pieces by carefully dabbing on fresh glaze with a finger or small brush.

If the glaze is just too poorly applied, scrape it all off, wash the piece, let it dry, and start over again.

TERRA SIGILLATA

The use of this refined clay slip can give a sculpture a shiny quality without glazing.

To make terra sigillata, mix about 500 grams of a fine-grained red earthenware, such as Cedar Heights Redart, into a liter of water. Add 1 cc of deflocculant (either soda ash or Calgon) and let everything sit for about 15 minutes. Shake the mixture vigorously and let it settle for at least 24 hours. Pour off everything, except the heaviest material, into another container. Discard the sludge. Remix the saved portion and allow it to settle for another day. Pour off the top two-thirds of the mixture into a flat pan and let the water evaporate. To ensure fine, even grain, grind the dry terra sigillata with a mortar and pestle and pass it through an 80-mesh or finer sieve.

APPLICATION

Mix a 50-50 batch of powder with water to make a thin slip. Brush or spray an even coating on leather-hard clay. As soon as it has dried, burnish the coating with the back of a spoon or a smooth rock lubricated with a few drops of cooking oil for a harder, glossier finish.

COLORS

Natural terra sigillata will fire from red to brown in oxidation, and black in reduction. Other colors can be developed by adding 3 to 10 percent of a colorant, such as copper carbonate, cobalt carbonate or ceramic body stain, to 30 percent dry terra sigillata and 70 percent water.

FIRING

Fire the dry coated ware to cone 06 (991° C/1816° F) or below for best color and a shiny surface. Higher firing will dull the surface. Properly fired terra sigillata will have the appearance of glaze, but the ware will not be waterproof.

Delicate sgrafitto decoration accents the terra sigillata surface of *Souls May Travel in Odd Vessels*. Roberta Kaserman, 1988. Unglazed porcelain, terra sigillata, gouache, wood, 24 x 19 x 20″ (61 x 48.1 x 50.8 cm). Photograph: David L. Brown.

Terra sigillata can also be used on lowfire clay.
Gary Bloom, *Waterways*, 1987.
Unglazed whiteware, terra sigillata, wood, plastic
doll, 14 x 16 x 4½″ (35.6 x 40.6 x 11.4 cm).
Photograph: David L. Brown.

The oldest and best known self-glazing material is referred to as
Egyptian paste. This type of modeling paste is usually made of silica,
sand and certain glaze compounds, with very little actual clay as part of
its make up. As a completed sculpture dries, the soluble glaze salts rise
to the surface and cover the entire object with a fine, fuzzy coating.
When fired, the coating forms a glaze.

SELF-GLAZING CLAYS

FORMING

Egyptian paste gives best results when hand modeled by pinch, coil or
slab methods. Wheel work is difficult because the paste is not very
plastic. Slip casting allows the soluble salts to leach into the mold and
clog its pores, rendering it useless. Simple press molds can be used if
the paste object is removed as soon as possible. This allows the salts to
form a proper surface coating.

HANDLING

Dry mix the paste ingredients and keep them in a covered container. Add water to only enough material to be used at one time. The paste dries fairly rapidly and if left standing, the salts will disassociate from the paste. Keep work in progress lightly misted with water to prevent the salts from forming too soon. When work is complete, leave the sculpture uncovered for at least 3 days to assure complete drying. Do not touch the paste — finger marks will prevent the salts from fully blooming on the surface.

COLOR

Two to 5 percent of copper carbonate added to a base paste will give the familiar turquoise color; 1 to 2 percent of cobalt carbonate gives a rich blue. For purple tones, add 1 to 3 percent of manganese carbonate. Ten percent of almost any ceramic body stain will impart a bright color. The color effects will depend upon the base paste and the firing temperature. Make and fire test samples first. **Because the paste is slightly caustic, always wash hands thoroughly after working.**

FIRING

Fire Egyptian paste in an oxidation atmosphere. Support objects on Kanthal wire stilts to prevent the glaze from sticking to kiln shelves. To further protect shelves, coat them with a flint and kaolin wash. After the wash has dried, dust on a coating of powdered whiting.

Fire the kiln slowly, particularly if the sculptures are solid. Fire accurately to the recommended temperature. Underfiring will give poor colors and a rough surface. Overfiring will cause the paste to bubble or melt.

Commercially prepared Egyptian pastes and other self-glazing clays are available. For best results, follow all the recommendations outlined above.

This sculpture was made with self-glazing clay.
Ann Christenson, *Persona*, 1984.
Mid-range self-glazing clay, steel,
28 x 8½ x 9″ (71.1 x 21.6 x 22.9 cm).
Photograph: Ben Blackwell.

American raku developed from the methodical, introspective, almost religious Japanese method of firing to become a relatively inexpensive, fast and exciting technique. It has become a way to imbue sculptures with lustrous and elusive colors and impart a desirable smoky blackness to the clay.

CLAY

Almost any clay body can be used for raku, as long as it has a sufficient amount of coarse-grained clay in it. Stonewares, porcelains or high fire-clay bodies with additions of up to 40 percent grog, sand or sawdust work well.

Works may be constructed with any clay forming method. Take care not to make walls too thick or too thin. Avoid severely constricted forms, and join all parts securely. Poorly made objects will not withstand the shock of the firing method.

GLAZES

Because raku glazes must be able to mature at very low temperatures, they must also have high thermal resistance to prevent **crawling** or other flaws from occurring. The fast firing process often prevents all the materials in a glaze from fully maturing. **Although lead is no longer widely used in raku glazes, other partially combined compounds could cause toxic illness if ingested over a period of time.**

The usual oxide colorants can be used effectively in raku glazes. Antimony and chrome oxides can give reds and oranges in oxidation. Silver nitrate and copper chloride create lustrous qualities. Copper carbonate, gives deep reds and metallic golds in reduction.

Apply the glazes thickly and allow them to fully dry before firing. Preheat glazed ware to prevent the glaze from falling off after being placed in the kiln.

SAFETY EQUIPMENT

Use long, sturdy metal tongs to manipulate ware in the kiln. Use a metal hook to open and close the kiln door. Wear approved heat-resistant long gloves to protect hands and arms. Wear #5 or #6 welder's goggles to protect the eyes. Use metal, not plastic, cans for water and

Jerry L. Caplan, *Knight*.
Raku fired clay, nails,
20″ (50.8 cm) tall.

combustible materials. **Have a garden hose or fire extinguisher handy in case of an emergency.**

KILN

The kiln should be fairly small to allow rapid heat buildup between firing cycles. The larger the kiln, the longer it will take to reheat. For best results, use a fuel kiln to gain initial reduction effects on clay and glazes. Make sure the door opens easily and shuts tightly. Have spy holes of adequate size to easily check the fire as it progresses.

Electric kilns can be used for raku as well. **Shut off power each time the kiln is to be opened. Inserting metal tongs into an electrified kiln could be FATAL.**

Ceramic fiber kilns are rapidly replacing firebrick kilns for use in raku. The light weight and easy portability of some styles provide easy access to the ware. Because the kiln itself heats and cools rapidly, the firing can actually be stopped between loads.

FIRING

Although it is possible to single-fire raku ware, kiln losses can be reduced if pieces are bisque fired first. Preheat the kiln. While wearing gloves and goggles, grasp the sculpture carefully but firmly with the tongs and place it in the kiln.

Depending upon their composition, most raku glazes begin to mature within 3 to 30 minutes. Check the firing often by looking through the spy holes. When the glaze has stopped bubbling and has taken on a smooth, glassy look, quickly remove the ware with tongs.

For oxidation effects, allow the ware to cool uncovered or dunk it in water. To attain secondary reduction smoking effects, place the glowing ware into a metal container half full of combustible material such as

A variation on raku firing — this work was low fired with no glaze and then reduced in a container of sawdust and newspaper.
Etta Winigrad, *Antagonists*.
Smoke-fired whiteware,
7 x 4 x 27″ (17.8 x 10.2 x 68.6 cm).
Photograph: the artist.

sawdust, dry leaves or grass. Add more combustibles and cover the container with a metal lid. Allow the piece to reduce for 5 to 20 minutes to thoroughly blacken the clay and enhance glaze effects. Remove the work from the container and allow it to cool naturally or quench it in water.

Susan and Steven Kemenyffy, *The Indianapolis Lady,* 1987.
Reduction fired raku clay, lusters,
4 x 2½ x ⅔′ (1.2 x .8 x .2 m).
Photograph: JL Color, Erie, PA.

SALT/ VAPOR GLAZING

Common salt has been used as a material for glazing ceramics for centuries. The traditional **salt glazing** process is conducted as a high temperature single firing. When the desired temperature is reached, loads of salt are shoveled into the kiln. The salt immediately volatilizes, combining with the raw clay to form a glass on all exposed surfaces. If there is not enough water vapor present to combine with the hydrochloric acid produced, chlorine gas is formed. **If inhaled, chlorine gas settles in the lungs causing severe damage and possible death. Salt glaze in a very well ventilated area or outdoors.**

A safer and more economical method of vapor firing is known as **soda firing.** The technique is similar to that of traditional salt glazing except that soda ash or bicarbonate of soda is used as the glazing material instead of salt. The result by-product of this firing is carbon dioxide, which is considerably less harmful than chlorine gas. **However, fumes from soda firing can irritate eyes, nose and throat.** As an added bonus, soda firing can be conducted at much lower temperatures.

KILN

It is wise to have a separate kiln for vapor glazing because the vapors produced during firing coat all exposed surfaces, including kiln walls and shelves. In subsequent fires, the glaze on the walls and shelves revaporizes throughout the kiln. Although vapor from soda ash does not deteriorate kiln materials as rapidly as salt, it is a good idea to protect the walls with a coating of aluminum oxide. Coat silicon carbide shelves with a wash of alumina hydrate before each firing.

Akio Takamori, *Human*, 1987.
Salt glazed porcelain, overglazes,
19 x 27 x 8″ (48.3 x 68.6 x 20.3 cm).
Courtesy: Garth Clark Gallery, New York and Los Angeles.

Robert M. Winokur, *Parquet Floor or Wall. Table Series*, 1987.
Salt glazed stoneware, ash glaze, slips, engobes, 4½ x 32 x 22″ (11.4 x 81.3 x 55.9 cm).
Photograph: Steve Winokur/Mike Winokur.

FIRING

When stacking the kiln, place several small rings of clay near a spy hole. These will be used as **draw trials** to check the amount of glaze being deposited on the ware.

During a vapor firing, regular stilts will become glaze coated and rendered useless. To help prevent the clay from sticking to the kiln shelves, place several small balls of clay rolled in flint under each work to be fired.

A vapor firing proceeds like any other single fire cycle. Warm the kiln slowly to allow chemically combined water to escape and organic materials to burn out. At cone 017 (727° C/1341° F), put the kiln into a light to medium reduction to enhance color. Continue to fire in reduction until the desired temperature is reached. Cones are no longer effective after the first salting. If accuracy is necessary, use a pyrometer.

For an even glaze coat, throw measured scoops of soda ash into each salting port. After ten minutes, hook out a draw trial, quench it in water and examine the glaze. Continue this procedure until the desired glaze effect is achieved. About two-thirds of a pound (300 g) of soda ash for each cubic foot (.03 m³) of kiln space is reasonable to start with for an average firing. Make appropriate adjustments according to taste. For random flash effects, throw several handfuls of soda ash into the kiln at short intervals. To enhance oxide decorations, vapor glazing can also be done in oxidation.

OVERGLAZE DECORATION

When a sculpture has cooled from its final glaze firing, certain lower temperature techniques can be used to bring about further enhancement. After these applications have been completed, the work is then refired to the appropriate temperature.

CHINA PAINT

Historically, china painters ground their own private mixtures of colorants with exotic oils to create brilliant color highlights on fired ware. Today, there are many companies which offer a vast array of luminous colors which can be applied directly from jar or tube, more commonly known as overglazes.

APPLICATION

First, use denatured alcohol or acetone (**both of which can be toxic**) to thoroughly clean the object. Apply the paint very thinly and evenly.

Bright overglaze colors stand out against the matt black setting of this work.
Les Lawrence. *Tea Set in Wall Shrine.*
Stoneware, overglaze,
18 x 18″ (45.7 x 45.7 cm).
Photograph: John Dixon.

Do not go over freshly painted areas. Use only fine quality camel hair brushes for lines. To cover large areas, use a good quality air brush. Paint applied too thickly will crawl or fall off when fired. Clean off mistakes immediately with a cotton swab dipped in alcohol. For more precise cleaning, wait until the paint is completely dry and scrape off the excess with a single-edged razor blade.

FIRING

Most china paints fire in oxidation to the cone 019 to 014 (668°–834° C/ 1234°–1533° F) range. Many colors have an extremely short range and can burn out with as little as a 10° overfiring. In many cases a second application and firing are needed to bring out the best color. Follow manufacturer's recommendations.

Luster glazes are actually thin metallic overlays which are fired onto the surface of a glaze. Although it is possible to prepare lusters in the studio, several companies offer ready-to-use metallic, pearlescent and bright metal lusters. Commercial lusters are in suspension and are not dissolved mixtures. The containers should not be shaken and any residue at the bottom should be discarded.

LUSTER GLAZE

APPLICATION

Work with lusters in an adequately ventilated area. Wear an approved vapor respirator (not just a paper mask). Lusters contain toluene, chloroform and other possibly toxic materials. Apply lusters to a clean, dry and dust-free surface. Lusters can be applied by pouring or dipping, provided that the coating is quite thin. For interesting mottled effects, lusters can be applied by sponging. Cut off a portion of a clean natural sponge, dip it into the luster and gently dab it onto the glazed surface. Discard the sponge after use.

Intricate designs are accentuated by the use of lusters. Jillian Barber, *Oriental Mask,* 1984. Glazed whiteware, underglazes, lusters, 18 x 14″ (45.7 x 35.6 cm). Photograph: Martin Doyle.

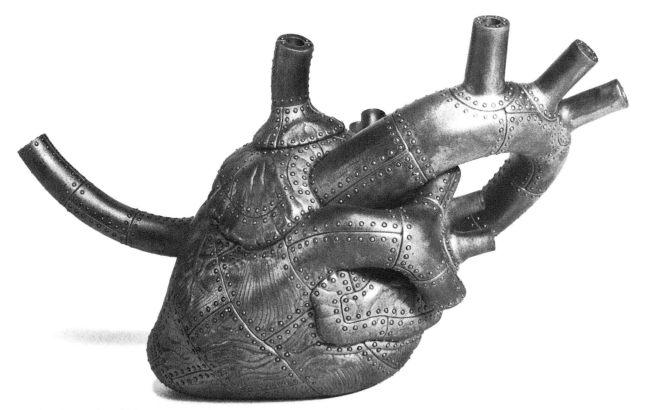

A galvanized steel-like appearance
results from using silver grey luster on
unglazed fired clay.
Richard T. Notkin, *Heart Teapot:
Ironclad — Yixing Series*, 1987.
Unglazed slipcast stoneware, luster,
6⅛ x 11⅝ x 4⅝″ (15.6 x 29.5 x
11.8 cm). Courtesy: Garth Clark
Gallery, New York and Los Angeles.
Photograph: the artist.

Use only fine camel hair brushes for lines or small areas. To prevent
contamination, each color should have its own brush. Do not reapply
luster to a freshly coated surface. Too thick an application can cause
the luster to powder off after firing. For larger areas, use a good quality
airbrush. To prevent spitting, frequently clean the tip of the airbrush
with acetone. Clean brushes and airbrush thoroughly with acetone after every use.

FIRING

Luster glazes must be fired in an oxidation atmosphere. Insufficient oxygen will give a cloudy appearance or cause discoloration. **Fire with a
well ventilated kiln. Lusters release toxic fumes in the early firing
stages.**
  Most lusters mature at cone 020 to 018 (625°–696° C/1157°–1285° F).
Overfired lusters can change color or burn out.

After the kiln is stacked with ware at least 1 inch (2.54 cm) apart, fire slowly to about 450° C (842° F) with the kiln door ajar to ensure the complete burning of all organic materials and carbon. Close the door and slowly fire the kiln to the desired temperature. Keep the spy holes open throughout the firing to ensure sufficient oxygen. When temperature has been reached, close the spy holes, shut off the kiln and let it cool slowly. To prevent the ware from splitting, wait until the kiln is cold before unstacking. Several reapplications and refirings will greatly enhance the depth of color with luster glazes.

Onglaze lithographs or watermount decals, are images printed in ceramic glazes on special paper and lacquer coated to preserve the image during application. Many manufacturers publish catalogs with thousands of images ready for use.

DECALS

APPLICATION

Thoroughly clean and dry the glazed surface to be decorated. Cut out the desired decal from its mounting sheet and place it in a pan of room temperature water. Allow only enough time for the paper to become completely soaked. Drain the decal and then lay it on the object. Slide the backing paper out from under the decal and make final position adjustment. Use a rubber squeegee or stiff piece of cardboard to force all water and air bubbles from the center of the decal outward. Dab excess water with a dry cloth. If the decal is not completely adhered to the glaze in this manner, it will fire poorly.

FIRING

Fire decals in the same manner as luster glazes. Most decals mature at the same temperature as lusters. Follow manufacturer's recommendations.

Author, *Spirit of '76 Drum Cookie Jar.*
Glazed porcelain, overglaze, luster, decal,
7½ x 7½ x 7½" (19.1 x 19.1 x 19.1 cm).

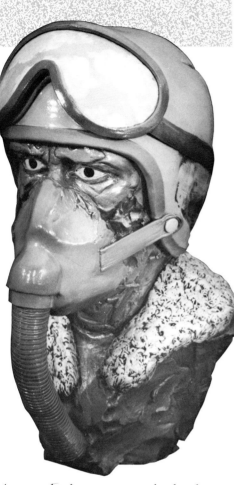

9 HEADS AND FIGURES

An example of a contemporary head sculpture. Joshua Nadel, *God is my co-pilot . . . but who the hell is the navigator.* Larger-than-life size. Glazed earthenware, underglazes.

Right:
A classical portrait bust.
Jean Jacques Caffieri, *Jean Baptiste Rousseau,* 18th century. Terra-cotta cast, 20¼ x 17 x 12″ (51.4 x 43.2 x 30.5 cm). Worcester Art Museum.

To best study the forms, masses and proportions of the head, use a live model. The nuances of individual expression and the subtle changes in form cannot be obtained from memory, plaster casts, or photographs. It is important to be able to view a three-dimensional head from many positions. Photographs give only the illusion of depth and do not allow sufficient viewpoints.

While it may be argued that certain heads make better subjects than others, the best choice is one that is willing to sit. It will take several sittings to do a portrait head accurately. The other essentials are a good supply of workable clay, some sort of modeling stand on which to place the work, an assortment of modeling tools and an armature to support the clay while it is being worked.

SCULPTING A HEAD

ARMATURES

Several types of armatures are commercially available but a simple head peg can be easily constructed. The baseboard should be a 12 inch (30.5 cm) square cut from ¾ inch (1.9 cm) plywood. Cut a 12 to 15 inch (30.4 to 38.1 cm) length of ¾ inch (1.9 cm) plumbing pipe and thread it on one end. Fit this into a pipe flange of the correct size. Screw or bolt the flange to the center of the base. Bend two lengths of Armaloy or other soft tubing to form loops about the size of a softball and stick the ends securely into the top of the vertical pipe. To help support the clay some sculptors affix a "butterfly" in the center of these loops. A butterfly is two short lengths of wood wired together in a cross. In the example, another butterfly has been placed to support the chin area.

The model should be seated on a comfortable chair or stool so that the head is at eye level. Arrange a head peg on a stand so that it is at the same level. Work from a standing position for ease of movement and viewpoint around both the model and sculpture.

Head peg with butterflies attached.

SOLID MODELING

Once the armature is in position, fill the cavity with clay until solid. Next, start building up a profile of the model. Press small strips or balls of soft clay onto the base form, carefully observing the model. Construct the profile as if making a silhouette. Note the angle of the throat and chin and transfer this to the clay form. While adding bits of clay, continue to check the relationship of the chin to nose and lips.

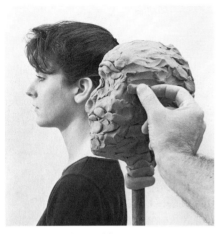

Building up the profile.

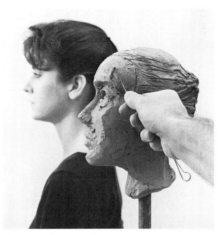

Carving planes and curves.

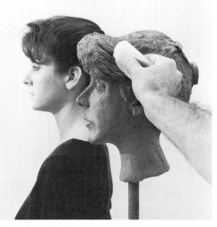

Detailing the hair.

Completed portrait head with separate ponytail temporarily in place.

When this profile is satisfactory, reposition the workstand and build up the back profile. Remember to take the same care with the back of the head, noting how the base of the skull joins the neck. Use a paddle to compress the clay if needed. Then do the other side and finally the front. Continually move around the head doing quarter profiles as accurately as possible until the form is complete.

Continue to build up the general image of the head in this manner, working with the solid mass. Resist putting in details until the major proportions are correct. At this stage of the process form is all that should be considered. Remember Cézanne's theory that nature is made up of geometric forms. Carve or scrape away excess clay until the proper planes and curves are achieved.

Only after all the contours and planes of the head are accurately proportioned should details be introduced. Note from the front and side how the eyes fit into the skull. See how the upper and lower eyelids curve and tilt. Model each feature as carefully as possible, noting the proportions and relationships to the other features. Merely positioning the mouth correctly is not sufficient. Note how the lips bulge and curve. Observe how the corners of the mouth relate to the cheeks. View the model from above and from underneath as well as from the front and side positions.

Do not concentrate all the effort on the features, but keep working the whole head. This way, all the parts will remain in harmony with each other.

After the eyes have been blocked in, take time to align the ears. Work the back of the neck and hair. Then go back to the eyes and nose. Bring the detail up slowly around the whole head. Carefully carve or scrape surfaces until they mirror those of the model. Smearing water over the whole piece to make it "smooth" can ruin many hours of work. Often the natural textures of fingers and tools are far more dramatic than any applied textures.

Removing

Once the head has been satisfactorily completed, it must be allowed to stiffen before it can be removed from the armature. When it reaches this point, cut the head in half vertically behind the ears with a long knife or cutting wire. Carefully pull off the portions and set them on a cushioned surface. Hollow out each part to a thickness of ¼ to ½ inch (.64 to 1.27 cm). Join the parts securely, restore the surface over the seam line and let the head slowly dry.

Carving out the interior to ½″ (1.3 cm) thickness.

Portrait head sculpture. Note how glasses are represented. Juene Nowak Wussow, *The Dean of Art Teachers, Ed. Boerner.* Reduction fired unglazed stoneware, 18″ (45.7 cm) tall. Photograph: P. Richard Eells.

HOLLOW MODELING

Constructing a head with the hollow method should proceed in the same manner as solid modeling. The major difference is the way in which an armature is prepared. Nail or screw a 15 inch (38.1 cm) long 2 × 3 board vertically to the center of a 12 inch (30.5 cm) square base cut from ¾ inch (1.9 cm) plywood. Cover this head peg with tightly wadded newspaper to the approximate size of the head and neck. Tape a plastic bag over the paper.

Using strips or coils of clay, cover the paper form to gain the general shape of the model's head. Use the profile method, explained earlier, to build the portrait.

Fanciful sculpture of a hollow-formed slab-built head.
Francine Trearchis Ozereko, *Woman with Dog and Bird,* 1987.
Glazed earthenware, underglazes, slips, 38 x 17 x 10″ (96.5 x 43.2 x 25.4 cm).
Photograph: U. Mass. Photo Service.

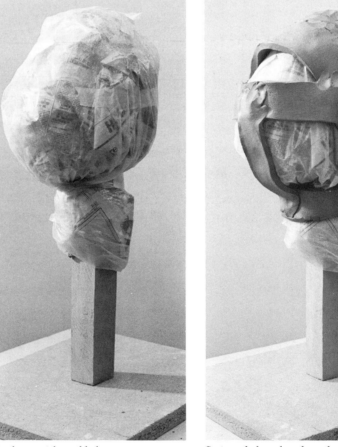

Head peg with wadded newspaper covered in plastic.

Strips of clay placed on the head peg.

Removing

After the head has stiffened, it can be easily taken off the wooden support, paper and all. If possible, remove the paper from inside. Otherwise, when the head is bisque fired, the paper will burn to ash and can later be shaken out.

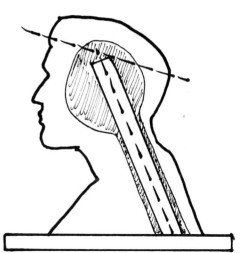

A variation of the head peg as used by Joshua Nadel for full busts. The vertical board is cut at a 10–15° angle, affixed to the base, wrapped with wadded paper and covered with plastic. The finished bust is cut into three parts (top, front, rear). After hollowing is completed, the parts are reassembled.

Frank Ozereko, *Roman Couple*, 1988.
Glazed terra-cotta, slips,
36 x 24 x 31″ (91.4 x 61 x 78.7 cm).
Photograph: U. Mass. Photo Service.

FIGURES

The only actual difference between sculpting heads and sculpting figures is one of scale. All the same techniques may be used to construct either subject. When making figures, however, the actual execution may require more thought and care.

Depending on the accuracy required, full figures can be modeled from memory with the use of a jointed mannequin (available from most art supply stores) or based on a live model.

If the finished piece is to be of moderate size, take the usual precautions of careful joining (allowing no entrapped air) slow drying and slow firing. If the figure is to be life-sized, pre-planning is a must. If kiln space is sufficient, the sculpture can be built and fired in one piece. If the kiln is not large enough to accommodate an entire figure, the sculpture must be made in parts which can be fitted together later.

Basil Racheotes, *Chief*, 1986.
Terra-cotta, powdered pigment patina, matt varnish, 14½ x 6 x 2¾" (36.8 x 15.2 x 7 cm).
Photograph: the artist.

Jointed wooden mannequin.

The fitted parts become an integral accent to this sculpture.
Eva Stettner, *Woman on Blue Stool*.
Raku fired clay, glaze, wooden stool,
59 x 36 x 36" (149.9 x 91.4 x 91.4 cm).
Photograph: Malcolm Varon.

Facing page:
Margaret Keelan, *Naomi III*, 1988.
Porcelain, paint,
13 x 8 x 5" (33 x 20.3 x 12.7 cm).
Photograph: Sidney Levine.

SECTIONAL CONSTRUCTION

A large or full-sized figure in a simple pose can often be built most easily from the ground up. Once the pose has been decided, work can start directly on a board or pallet strong enough to support the weight of the unfired piece. Sprinkle a coating of grog on the board to help keep the clay from adhering. Model the piece using whichever method seems appropriate, usually slab, coil or a combination of the two.

As the work progresses, keep the lower portions covered with plastic so that they will not dry too rapidly. To help prevent the work from collapsing, put wads of newspaper inside the form as the walls grow upward. The paper provides support, aids in moisture control and can be removed later or burned out during firing. Use temporary exterior props wherever needed during the early stages of construction. If the props are made of clay they can later be used to support the sculpture during firing.

When the maximum height of the section has been reached, lay plastic sheets around the rim to prevent the next section from sticking as construction proceeds. Place the next coil or slab directly on top of the rim as usual and continue to build upward. An interior flange can

Completed work installed at Ark Park, Lewiston, NY.
Gail Caulfield, *Art Parker,* 1987.
Glazed whiteware, glaze stains,
6′ (1.8 m) tall.
Photograph: Mel Schockner.

A sectional sculpture in progress. Note full-size drawings in background and props to hold leather-hard arm in position.

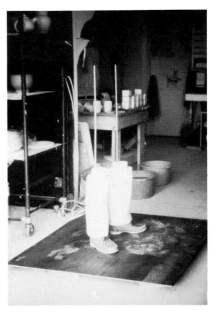

Fired legs in place. Note built-in pipe fitting flanges to support upper sections.

A large multi-unit floor and wall sculpture.
Jod Lourie, *Her Basic Assumption*, 1986.
Porcelain, 10 x 8 x 3′ (3 x 2.4 x .9 m).
Photograph: Clements and Howcroft.

Two views of one sculpture — with mask off and on.
Claudia Reese, *Cheetah Woman*, 1987.
Low-fired glazed stoneware, underglazes, sandblasted, 81 x 23 x 23″ (205.7 x 58.4 x 58.4 cm).
Photograph: Rick Patrick.

be added at the joint, if desired, to assure proper alignment and stability after the work has been fired.

Continue to construct the piece in this manner until it is completed. Allow the work to dry slowly in its assembled position to reduce any warping or twisting. When the sculpture is completely dry, separate the pieces carefully and fire them. After the work has been successfully fired, the sections can be restacked, glued or cemented, depending upon the final disposition of the sculpture.

10 PLASTER, MOLDS, AND MOLD-MAKING

Ten separate cast elements assembled into a specific design.
Richard T. Notkin, *Cube Skull Teapot (Variation #7) — Yixing Series*, 1987.
Unglazed slipcast stoneware,
5¼ x 4⅞ x 2⅞″ (13.3 x 12.4 x 7.3 cm).
Courtesy: Garth Clark Gallery, New York and Los Angeles. Photograph: the artist.

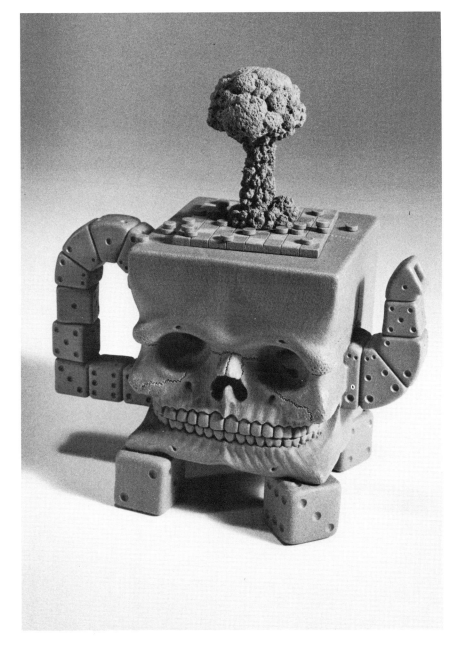

Plaster is quite useful in the ceramic sculpture studio. It can be used to make clay drying bats, bats for wheel work as well as molds for reproducing an object. However, plaster must be treated with a little respect. First, it is very important that plaster is never allowed to mix with clay. If this does happen and the clay is later fired, the bits of plaster will explode and damage the clay object. It is also important that powdered plaster is not allowed to become damp. If the plaster takes on too much atmospheric moisture, it will become grainy and hard to use. It could harden and be completely unusable. To reduce the possibility of these occurrences, always store plaster in airtight containers and be sure to clean the work area and equipment thoroughly after plaster has been used.

Plaster is pulverized gypsum that has been heated to drive off the chemically combined water. When water is added, the powder recrystallizes and becomes hard. Plaster is available in many grades of hardness. The most practical types for use in the clay studio are Industrial Molding Plaster and Number One Pottery Plaster. Either of these can be purchased most economically in 100 pound bags from building material suppliers. Both grades set quickly but still retain the ability to absorb moisture. Hardness and porosity are essential for plaster which is used in clay preparation and mold-making activities.

Casts made from molds of actual fruits.
Karen Thuesen Massaro, *Fruit Server #20.*
Glazed cast porcelain, underglaze,
3 x 10½ x 9½″ (7.6 x 26.7 x 24.1 cm).
Photograph: Lee Hocker.

MIXING

Sifting some plaster into a bucket of water until it looks right is standard procedure in most sculpture studios. Unfortunately, this method can give the plaster an uneven consistency which is detrimental to good mold work. For reliable results, add plaster to water by weight. Mix 100 pounds (45 kilograms) of plaster into 72 pounds (33 kilograms) of water. For smaller projects use a ratio of 3 pounds (1.35 kilograms) of plaster for every 1 quart (0.95 liter) of water.

Always add the plaster to the water, never add the water to the plaster. Sift the proper amount of plaster into the water, let it **slake,** or absorb water, for several minutes. Then stir from beneath the surface to release any air bubbles and remove lumps. Continue to stir until the plaster has reached pouring consistency. To test, simply draw a finger over the surface of the plaster. When the mark remains momentarily, the plaster is ready to pour.

Use room temperature water. Hot water will cause the plaster to stiffen before the water has been fully absorbed. Cold water will slow down the setting time and could give the plaster a granular consistency.

Waste plaster should never be poured into a sink. It will clog the drain pipes. The best method for disposing of leftover mixed plaster is to pour it into a heavy-duty trash bag. If a rubber or plastic mixing container is used, let the excess plaster harden first, then break out the hardened plaster and put it in the trash.

MAKING A DRYING BAT

Because hardened plaster will absorb moisture, it is an excellent material to use when drying or stiffening clay that is too soft for immediate use. For this reason, it is a good idea to have several drying bats in the studio.

First set up a wooden form of the appropriate size on a table or board with a smooth surface. Clamp the corners of the mold. Firmly press a coil of clay around the outside seams of the mold to prevent plaster from leaking when poured.

Apply commercial mold separator or undiluted dishwashing liquid to all surfaces the plaster will touch. Pour some dishwashing liquid onto a sponge, work it to a lather and stroke the lather all over the mold. Be sure to smooth away any bubbles; they can affect the surface of the final plaster piece. Apply the soap in several layers until a slick coating

Clamped wooden form sealed with clay coils.

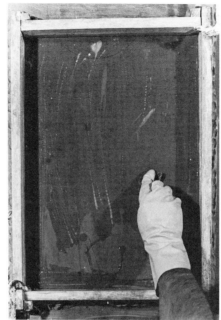

Applying mold separator to wooden form and table top.

Chicken wire placed in wooden form.

completely covers the mold. The mold will open easily later without damaging the plaster. Some sculptors use petroleum jelly as a separator. This is an acceptable substitute when used for bats and press molds. The jelly gets into the pores of the plaster, however, and will restrict the water absorption capability necessary for slipcasting molds. For added strength, place a piece of chicken wire or metal lath in the mold.

To determine the amount of water and plaster needed, measure the volume of the mold. In the example, the mold is 14 × 19½ × 1¾ inches (35.5 × 49.5 × 4.4 cm). Multiply these numbers together to derive the cubic measurement: 14 × 19.5 × 1.75 = 477.75 cubic inches. To find the quarts of water needed, divide this number by 81 (the approximate volume of a quart of plaster) 477.75 ÷ 81 = 5.89 quarts. To be sure there is enough material, round the total to 6 quarts. For the amount of dry plaster needed, multiply the figure by 3.0: 6 × 3.0 = 18 pounds (8.1 kilograms).

Pour 6 quarts of room temperature water into a large plastic container. Weigh out 18 pounds (8.1 kilograms) of plaster and sift it into the water. Let the mixture slake for about three minutes, then stir it continuously until the plaster has reached the proper consistency. Pour

Pouring the plaster.

Releasing the bat from the form.

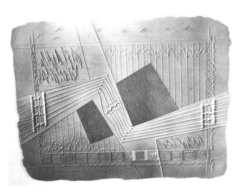
This slipcast wall relief was made by pouring slip onto incised plaster bat.
Jere Lykins, *Pagina A-21*.
Unglazed whiteware casting slip, gesso, acrylic paints, 16 x 22 x ¼″ (40.6 x 55.9 x .6 cm).
Photograph: the artist.

the plaster into the mold quickly but gently to avoid splashing. Immediately after the plaster is poured, jar the table or board several times to bring any air bubbles to the surface. Break the bubbles by blowing lightly on them. Allow the plaster to set untouched.

As plaster sets, a chemical change takes place, heat is given off and a slight expansion occurs. When the plaster has completely cooled, remove the mold. Because of excess moisture, the plaster will still feel damp to the touch. Put the bat aside in a warm place to allow it to dry completely before use. To prevent chipping, bevel all edges with a plaster rasp or Surform tool.

MAKING THROWING BATS

Make throwing bats with the same method used for drying bats. Use commercial bat rings, pie tins or pizza tins for different diameter bats. Soap the particular container thoroughly. Measure the plaster and water, using the same calculations used for drying bats. Pour the plaster and allow it to set. When the plaster has cooled, tap the back of the tin lightly and the bat will drop out. Bevel the edges of the bat.

Relief tile modeled in clay.

MAKING A ONE-PIECE PRESS MOLD

An easy way to reproduce relief tiles or other simple objects having no undercuts is by using a one-piece mold.

Model the relief tile from a solid block of clay. If there are undercuts in the design, the tile will not release from a mold. A slight upward taper to the design will also help ease removal of later casts.

When the original model is complete, set a wooden form around it with at least 1 inch (2.54 cm) clearance on each side, including the top. Clamp or tie the form and press a coil of clay into all the outside seams.

To determine the amount of plaster needed calculate the volume of the wooden mold. Measure or estimate the volume of the model. Subtract this amount from the mold volume. It is always prudent to make more plaster than calculated.

Apply separator carefully to all surfaces including the clay. Mix the plaster and pour it. Pour the excess into the pie tins to make extra bats. After the plaster has set, pull out the model and allow the mold to dry completely before use. Bevel the exterior edges and carefully carve away any unwanted **flashing,** or extended bits of plaster, from the interior of the mold.

Model placed into wooden form.

Finished plaster relief mold.

If a large number of objects is anticipated, make several molds. To preserve the model, bisque fire it before beginning the mold-making process. Be sure to soap the model well before each plaster pouring.

Using a One-Piece Press Mold

Once the mold has dried, push clay firmly into all parts of it. Check thickness by sticking a pin tool into the clay in various places and noting the depth. Add clay to low spaces and press down thick areas. After the mold has been filled satisfactorily, allow the clay to stiffen. The clay tile may also be waffle-cut to reduce weight and help prevent warping. Turn the mold over onto some wooden slats and let the clay continue to set up. After the clay has shrunk sufficiently, the tile will drop from the mold. Keep the tile on the slats so it dries evenly with less warping.

After several pressings, the mold may become too damp to let the clay stiffen quickly. Lightly brush some talc or baby powder into the mold before pressing more clay into it. This will help prevent the clay from sticking.

Pushing clay into mold. Note depression where relief is deepest to keep tile thickness even.

Cutting waffle pattern into reverse of tile.

A life-size plaster body cast was used to make the mold for this piece.
Gail Corcoran-Freundt, *New Wave Mermaid*, 1983.
Glazed stoneware, mixed media,
5 x 3′ x 7″. (1.5 x .9 m x 17.8 cm).
Photograph: the artist.

A press-molded figure, possibly representing Demeter, from the island of Rhodes. Sixth century BC, 5⅝ x 2¼ x 3⅜" (14.3 x 5.7 x 8.6 cm). Worcester Art Museum.

Clay model with parting line drawn on.

MAKING A TWO-PIECE MOLD

While a one-piece mold may be adequate for many relief forms and some simple sculptures, most three-dimensional works and objects with undercuts must be reproduced through the use of piece molds.

At first glance, many sculptures may appear too complex to reproduce with a two-piece mold. Upon careful examination a **parting line** can often be found. This line is the place where the front and back or top and bottom of the mold can be separated without damaging the sculpture. Sometimes it can be a straight line that evenly circumscribes the entire piece. More often the line must undulate over varying high points of the object.

Draw the parting line carefully over the surface of the model to be cast. Make sure the line is at the highest point of the plane and there are no accidental undercuts. Place the model in a position so that the line is as closely parallel to the tabletop as possible.

Build clay around the lower half of the model up to the parting line and at least one inch (2.54 cm) from all sides. Set up a wooden form around the object and the clay. Fill in any interior gaps with clay. Clamp or tie the form securely and fill the seams with clay. Sometimes a flexible form, or **cottle** — made of galvanized sheet metal, a strip of vinyl flooring or, in an emergency, a strip of corrugated cardboard — might fit better around the object. When the form is secure, soap all surfaces thoroughly. Calculate the volume of the mold, subtract the volume of the object, mix the plaster, and carefully pour without splashing or trapping air around the model.

After the plaster has set, turn the mold over and remove the built-up clay. Do not remove the model. To later align the mold halves, cut several **keys** into the plaster. Carve these indentations with a spoon or rounded knife edge to insure no undercuts. Reposition the mold form and secure it. Soap all surfaces well, especially the plaster half mold. Calculate, mix and carefully pour a new batch of plaster.

When the plaster has cooled, remove the mold form, separate the mold halves and take out the model. If done properly, the mold should separate easily and the model should come out with just a little effort. Allow the mold to dry. Bevel the outside edges. Carefully carve away any flashing from the mold cavity. In the example, clay was pressed into each half of the mold. The mold was squeezed together and the clay allowed to stiffen somewhat. The mold was opened and the form simply dropped out.

Clay built around lower half of model.

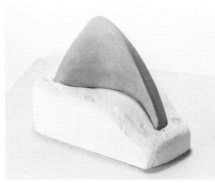

First half of mold with keys cut in.

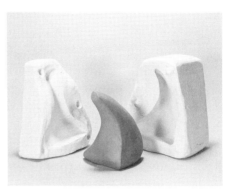

Completed mold.

Meghan Long, *Series #1*, 1989.
Glazed whiteware, marbled underglazes, each figure:
5½ x 4½ x 3½″ (14 x 11.4 x 8.9 cm).
Photograph: the author.

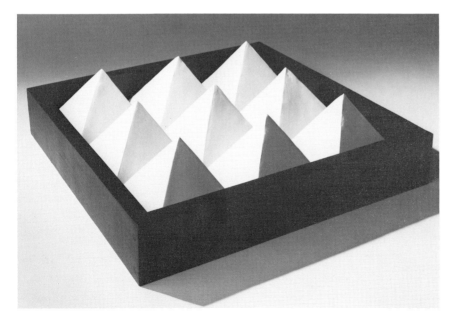

Press-molded pyramids.
John Rossetti, *Untitled #3*, 1987.
Low-fired stoneware, paint, wood,
16 x 16″ (40.6 x 40.6 cm).
Photograph: Ron White.

The finished work in place.
Mary Block. *Figure — Bott Home.*
Low-fired raku clay, lacquer,
5 x 4 x 2' (1.5 x 1.2 x .6 m).
Photograph: Marc Block.

MULTI-PIECE PRESS MOLDS

Some sculptural forms are too complex to be reproduced with a two-piece mold. In such instances, molds with many parts are needed. The more parts, the more difficult it will be to properly align and secure for use. After examination, it is sometimes easier to alter the original model slightly to make it work as a two-piece mold. If this is either not possible or not desired, then a multi-piece mold must be constructed.

In the example, the life-sized model was made of oil-based clay pressed over a metal armature. The advantage to using oil-based clay for the model is that it does not need to be constantly wet down to prevent shrinking or cracking. After the sculpture was satisfactorily completed, it was divided into workable areas by means of **shims.** These metal strips are cut from steel shim stock, readily available at good auto supply shops or industrial hardware stores. Galvanized sheet metal strips are also usable. Attention was paid to the accurate placement of the shims. Because each division acts as a parting line, under-cuts were to be avoided. The angle by which each mold piece was to be removed and replaced was also considered. Because plaster will not ad-

Life-size oil-based clay model ready to be cast.

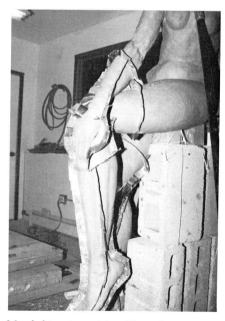

Metal shims in position. Note placement at highest point on each curve.

Plaster being applied to each section.

here to the oil-based clay or the metal shims, it was not necessary to soap either.

When all the shims were in place, enough plaster to fill one area at a time was mixed. In this case, the plaster was allowed to get somewhat thicker than for pouring so that it would not run when smeared on by hand and trowel. The model was covered from the bottom up. After the plaster had set, each section of the mold from the top down was carefully removed and the shims taken out. The interior of the mold sections were then thoroughly cleaned.

The plaster mold should be made at least 1 inch thick (2.54 cm). A layer or two of plaster gauze or regular burlap can be added for greater strength.

To use a multi-piece mold for pressing, force clay into each section of the mold. Continually check the clay wall thickness with a pin tool and make any appropriate adjustments. After the clay has reached the leather-hard stage, remove it from the mold sections. Assemble the clay pieces — over an armature if necessary — to check for proper fit. Make any necessary adjustments to the form. Let the clay dry slowly by covering it with plastic and then uncovering it for a few hours a day until it becomes bone dry.

Large scale works, such as the one shown, often need to be assembled over metal supporting structures after firing. By taking this into consideration during the early stages of design, the appropriate support mechanism can be prepared with little difficulty.

MOLDS FOR SLIP CASTING

A mold to be used for slip casting needs two things that a press mold does not require. The first is a hole into which the slip can be poured and the second is a reservoir to hold additional slip needed during the casting process. Both requirements are satisfied by the introduction of a **spare** into the mold.

Make the spare from clay or plaster into the shape of a truncated cone or plug. It is better to have a short, wide plug than a tall, thin one because the mold will have to be thicker on one side to accommodate the latter. Placement of the spare on the model depends upon the shape of the object to be cast. Be sure that the spare is on the upper surface of the mold and that it is level. If the model is made of wet clay, weld a clay plug onto it in the appropriate place. If the model is

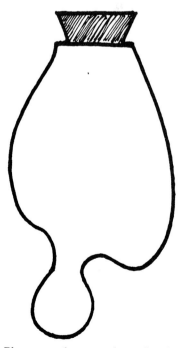

Placement of spare on base of model.

Slipcast parts made from actual objects.
Richard Shaw, *Mayonnaise Still Life*, 1988.
Porcelain casting slip, glazes, decal,
12 x 19 x 13″ (30.5 x 48.3 x 33 cm).
Courtesy: Braunstein/Quay Gallery.

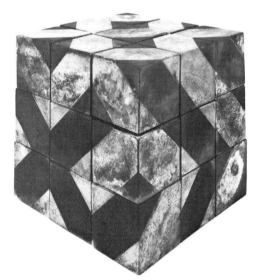

Slipcast multiples used in a single work.
Harriet E. Brisson, *27 Gold Cubes*.
Raku fired porcelain, each cube:
6 x 6 x 6″ (15.2 x 15.2 x 15.2 cm).
Photograph: Dennis Haggerty.

Large work cast from modeled parts.
Patti Warashina.
A Procession — 72 N.W. Artists.
Glazed whiteware, underglaze, mixed media,
8 x 3 x 10′ (2.4 x .9 x .3 m).
Location: Seattle Opera House.
Photograph: Roger Schrieber.

plaster or another hard material, use white glue to affix a plaster spare in its proper position. The spare can be removed, if need be, after the mold is finished.

Proceed to make a mold in the same manner as a two-piece press mold. Draw a parting line, set up the model in a horizontal position, secure the cottle, soap, calculate the amount of plaster needed, mix and pour the first half. After the mold has set, turn it over and remove the clay walls. It is essential to cut keys to insure proper alignment. Secure the cottle, soap all the surfaces, calculate, mix and pour again.

To extend the use of a casting mold, make the walls at least 2 inches thick (5.08 cm) on all sides. While this adds weight to the mold, it allows for a greater number of casts to be made before the mold becomes too wet to work well. When this occurs, assemble the mold, put it in a warm place and allow it to thoroughly dry before reusing. If the mold is left open to dry it could warp and be rendered useless.

PRODUCTION MOLDS

When a great number of objects are to be reproduced, several identical molds are required. It is possible to use the original model over and over again if it has not been damaged. For greater accuracy in each mold, it is better to make molds of the original model mold. This is known as the **block and case** method — a master mold of each piece of the model mold is made and then cast in plaster. This technique is somewhat complicated and time consuming. For best results, seek a professional mold maker.

If a handforming clay is thinned with so much water that it can be poured, it will sink to the bottom of the container in a clump. A clay suitable for casting has to be deflocculated with sodium silicate or Calgon. Most studio clays can be converted for casting. Because many good quality casting slips are commercially available, this is usually not necessary. Stonewares, earthenwares and porcelains can be obtained in different colors and can be fired through a wide range of temperatures.

Secure the parts of the slipcasting mold together with heavy rubber bands, rope or commercial nylon straps. Stir the slip well and strain it through a 60-mesh sieve to remove any lumps. Pour the slip into the mold to the top of the spare.

Clay adheres to the inside of the mold and begins to form the wall of the object as the mold absorbs water from the slip. After 5 minutes, check the thickness of the wall by cutting into the clay wall in the spare. When the wall has become the desired thickness, pour out the remaining slip and invert the mold over a container to fully drain. In about 3 minutes, turn the mold upright and check it. If the shine has gone from the clay, cut away the excess from the side of the spare.

Let the form set up in the mold for at least 20 minutes. Taking the form out of the mold too soon will cause it to slump, either as it dries or when it is fired. If left in the mold too long, the form could crack. These times are generalizations. The actual time depends on the slip used, the thickness and wetness of the mold, and the studio humidity.

SLIP CASTING

The colored inlaid pieces are placed into the mold before the object is cast.
Kathy Erteman, *Table Vessel*, 1986.
Partially glazed porcelain, glaze stains, glass cane, 14 x 9 x 9″ (35.6 x 22.9 x 22.9 cm).
Photograph: Michele Maier.

Limited edition slipcast figure. Left to right: separately cast bowl, glaze finished piece, assembled piece prior to glazing.
Elee Koplow. *The Festival Lady*, © 1984.
Glazed whiteware, underglazes,
15 x 6 x 6″ (38.1 x 15.2 x 15.2 cm)
Photograph: Marc Malin.

11 FIRING

Ruth Rippon, *The Lollies*.
Reduction-fired stoneware, engobes. Life-size.
Installed: The Pavilions, Sacramento, CA.
Collection: Robert Powell.

A kiln is basically a box insulated to hold heat. Ceramic objects are placed into this box and heat is introduced. Kilns can be fired with anything from wood to oil, gas, electricity or even cow dung. The two major heat sources in use today are gas (natural or bottled) and electricity. Although the goal is the same — to heat clay to its maturity — each requires its own type of kiln.

ELECTRIC KILNS

Availability and variety of commercially manufactured electric kilns has made them the major type of kiln used in the United States. They are simple to install and maintain. They are also efficient and relatively inexpensive to purchase and operate.

Electric kilns are manufactured in two versions: frontloading and toploading. Frontloading kilns have a swinging or sliding door on one side to facilitate stacking. Toploaders have a lid that can be raised manually or by a pulley. Both types of kiln are insulated with either firebrick, glass fiber block or blanket — or a combination of the two. For most applications related to sculpture, either material is satisfactory.

Top loading electric kiln. Skutt. Model 1027.

There are, however, minor disadvantages to each kind of kiln. Front-loaders are generally more expensive because of the bracing needed to support the door and are also often quite heavy. Stacking the kiln shelves can be somewhat awkward. Toploaders tend to cool more rapidly than heavily insulated frontloaders although manufacturers are hard at work to correct this situation and still maintain relative portability. Because shelves are lowered into position, tall works are sometimes damaged and bits of debris can fall unnoticed on objects below. The ease and low expense with which these kilns can be fired far offsets these small drawbacks.

An electric kiln is heated by metal elements placed in grooves within its walls. When electricity is passed through them, the elements generate heat much like a light bulb. Several grades of elements are available. A well-insulated kiln equipped with top grade elements capable of attaining high temperatures is the best investment.

Safety
Although there is no danger of blowout or fire as with fuel kilns, to avert potential hazards, set up an electric kiln on a level cement floor at least 12 inches (30.4 cm) from any walls or equipment. If the floor

Bailey walk-in front loading kiln.

is wood, elevate the kiln on concrete blocks to increase air circulation underneath. Protect the floor with fireproof material.

Sufficient electrical power must be available for the kiln. Be certain that the line specifications are adequate for the kiln's requirements. It is often best to install a separate line and circuit breaker system directly "from the street" rather than relying on existing lines in the building. Metering is expensive and really only necessary in schools or commercial operations. Costs can be estimated by multiplying the kilowatt rating by the local unit cost and multiplying this by the firing time.

Proper kiln ventilation is essential. Every time the kiln is fired, toxic fumes, gases, heat and smoke are released into the surrounding atmosphere. Several kinds of exhaust hoods and kiln venting systems are now commercially available. It is strongly recommended that such a system be installed.

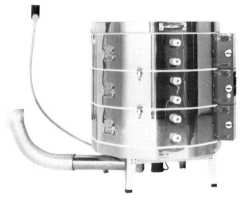

Skutt "EnviroVent" kiln ventilation system shown installed on Model 1227 kiln.

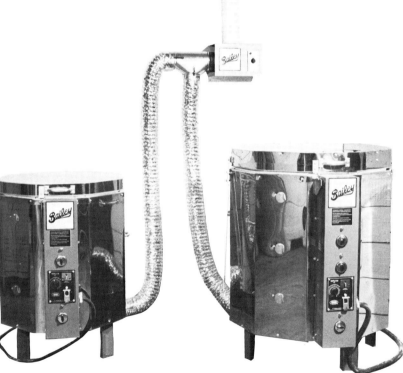

Bailey Fume-Vent System

FUEL KILNS

Clayworkers have settled on two basic types of design for fuel burning kilns: **updraft** and **downdraft.** An updraft kiln has the flame enter from under the ware and exit above. The flame in a downdraft kiln usually enters from the sides, is forced to the top of the kiln and then downward to exit through a flue at the rear of the kiln.

Two styles of kiln are also useful for studio firing: the **sprung arch** and the **catenary arch.** The sprung arch kiln is a firebrick box with a curved roof held together with a metal frame. The catenary arch is a self-supporting firebrick kiln curving directly from the floor, requiring no additional bracing. Both styles of kiln can be constructed in almost any size and adapted to almost any source of fuel.

Plans for constructing these and other types of fuel burning kilns are readily available through ceramic periodicals and in books devoted to the subject. Consult people who have built kilns to seek solutions to problems before they arise. Commercial fuel kilns are available, but many of them, although quite efficient and safe, are cost prohibitive.

Gas-fired raku kiln built by Penelope Fleming. Double-hinged door swings hot-face away when opened.

Schematic of updraft kiln showing heat circulation.

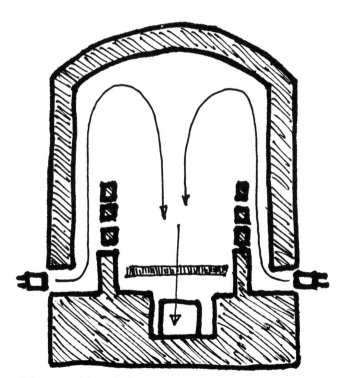

Schematic of downdraft kiln showing heat circulation.

Catenary arch kiln, 40 cubic foot capacity, gas fired. Courtesy: Roger Harvey. Photograph: Felicity Craven.

Safety

Ventilation is of prime importance when firing fuel kilns. The release of noxious gases, smoke and heat accompanies every firing. If the kiln is not situated outdoors, away from buildings and vegetation, it should have a sheet metal hood over it with an exhaust stack exiting the building.

Construct the kiln on a level cement floor. Have at least 2 feet (61 cm) of space between the kiln, the walls and any other equipment.

Proper emergency shut-offs must be built into any gas burner system. Check them periodically to see that they work. Keep dry powder fire extinguishers charged and nearby.

Wear appropriate fire retardant clothing, gloves and face shields when firing a fuel kiln. Remember flame temperatures can reach in excess of 1400° C/2552° F.

Sprung arch kiln, 40 cubic foot capacity, gas fired. Courtesy: Gerry Williams. Photograph: the author.

After time, effort and inspiration have been expended on creating a sculpture in clay, it could be disastrous to leave the work in its fragile condition. To protect the work from untimely demise, the clay must be fired. During firing, certain chemical changes take place which permanently transform the clay. Both atmospheric and chemically combined water are driven from the clay, organic compounds decompose and alumina and silica combine. All of these changes contribute toward strengthening the clay and turning it into a rock-like substance.

When clay is being fired, the heat must rise at a rate slow enough to allow time for these changes to take place properly. The cooling cycle must also proceed slowly to prevent sudden chemical reversals which will cause the clay to crack. Firing in a well insulated kiln will help regulate these cycles.

KILN FURNITURE

Unless the sculpture is so large that it just fits into the kiln, some sort of shelving and supports are usually needed to stack objects in a kiln. For moderately sized works that are of reasonable weight, kiln shelves made of refractory clay are sufficient. These products come in different sizes and shapes and can be fired in oxidation to cone 10 (1285° C/ 2345° F) with little warping.

For heavier objects fired at high temperatures in reduction, silicon carbide shelves must be used. They are thicker and stronger than refractory shelves, have greater thermal conductivity and are resistant to failure in reduction atmosphere. However, constant use in oxidizing firings will cause silicon carbide shelves to fail.

Refractory clay kiln posts are available in different sizes. When stacking a kiln, use posts of appropriate height so that the shelves are safely

Refractory kiln bars, pins and tile shelves used to support works being fired. Do not exceed manufacturers' maximum temperature when firing with these items.

clear of the ware. Hard firebrick **soaps** (9 × 2½ × 2¼″/23 × 6 × 6 cm) can also be used as kiln posts, especially for reduction firing.

Tile setters, stilts, pins and other accessories can be used to aid in stacking tiles or small, completely glazed objects. Many of these accessories are designed to perform only at low temperatures. Heed manufacturer's recommendations.

KILN WASH

To protect shelves from accidental glaze drips, coat the tops with kiln wash. Dry mix equal parts (by weight) of flint and kaolin with about a 2 percent addition of bentonite. Mix with water to a creamy consistency. Using a paint roller or wide brush, evenly spread the wash onto the shelves. Be careful not to drip or coat the sides or bottom. The kiln wash might flake off during firing and spoil glazes below. For new shelves, apply several coats, allowing one to dry before adding the next. Premixed kiln wash can also be purchased.

Touch up any chips after each firing to preserve the surface. If the buildup becomes too uneven, scrape off all the kiln wash and reapply. If glaze has dripped onto a shelf, carefully chip it off with a chisel. Keep the chisel at an acute angle to the shelf and tap with a hammer. If an entire piece has stuck to the shelf, grasp it and then lightly strike the shelf around it with a wooden or rubber mallet. Do not hit the sculpture. Depending upon the value of the work, it is sometimes better to risk breaking the shelf. Keep tapping around the piece until it comes free. Patch or replace the kiln wash. Grind off the unwanted glaze from the object.

Another way to prevent glaze from sticking to a kiln shelf is to dust it with a coating of **alumina hydrate.** The powder also acts as a cushion allowing clay objects to move more freely as they shrink during firing. Grog sprinkled over a shelf will also act as a cushion for works as they shrink. However, it will not protect the shelf from glaze drips.

PYROMETRIC CONES

To determine when the proper temperature of a firing has been reached, use pyrometric cones. Cones are elongated, pyramid shaped objects made of controlled clay bodies designed to fuse at specific temperatures. In the United States, Orton cones are the generally accepted standard. They are available as large or small cones and also in a self-

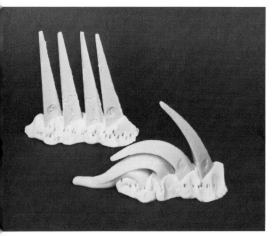

Pyrometric cone pats: unfired, fired. Two guide cones, desired temperature cone, guard cone shown.

supporting version. These cones measure heat work, or the time/temperature effect when firing ceramics.

It is good practice to set three consecutively numbered large cones side by side in a plaque or pat of clay. The lower temperature **guide cone** is placed to the left, the **desired temperature cone** in the center and a higher temperature **guard cone** to the right. Set the cones in the clay pat at an angle of 8 degrees with their stamped numbers facing outward. Punch small holes in the clay pat to allow complete drying and prevent explosion in the fire.

During firing, each cone begins to bend as it nears its specific fusion point. When the tip of the guide cone has bent to the level of its base, check the kiln often until the firing cone is fully bent. Shut off the kiln and let it slowly cool. Do not reuse unbent cones, they are no longer accurate.

While stacking a kiln, place cone pats so they can be easily seen through the spyholes. In large or multilevel kilns, set cones near each spyhole to help detect possible uneven heating.

In the higher heat ranges, cones can be difficult to see. **Use Number 5 or 6 welder's goggles to aid in seeing the cones and protecting the eyes.**

Small cones perform the same function as large ones but fire about 14° C/25° F hotter at each setting. Small cones are also used as the trigger for electric kiln shut-off equipment. Pyrometric bars are specifically designed for this purpose.

AUTOMATIC CONTROLS

Many kinds of automatic temperature control devices, preprogrammed mechanical or computerized panels and timed and/or cone triggered shut-offs are available. While all serve their intended function, none are guaranteed. Use caution and do not rely solely on mechanical means when firing a kiln.

STACKING THE KILN

When placing sculptures into a kiln, set them in the center of the shelves to aid in even heat absorption. Set each shelf with three evenly spaced posts for stable three-point support. Stack each set of posts directly over the set beneath to insure rigidity. For good heat distribution, allow at least 1 inch (2.54 cm) of clearance between the top of an object and the next shelf.

Dawson Kiln Sitter, Model LT-3-H with both cone and timer shut-offs.

Large sections of a sculpture stacked in a kiln before firing. Note smaller sections placed inside larger ones supported by pieces of glass fiber blanket.
Above right:
The completed sculpture.
Brian Buckley. *Wednesday and Thursday*, 1985. Low-fired stoneware, Styrofoam, paint, each piece: 75 x 36 x 14″ (190.5 x 91.4 x 35.6 cm). Photograph: the artist.

If a shelf post wobbles or a shelf is not quite level, roll a small pat of fireclay onto some flint. Stick the fireclay onto the bottom of the post and firmly set it in place. After the firing, the clay can be removed easily.

BISQUE FIRE

A clay sculpture can be safely fired up to its maturing temperature in a single firing provided that the heat is increased very slowly. Depending upon the size of the work and its thickness, such a firing could take several days.

The general practice of two firings is recommended. This procedure allows easier handling of the object providing an opportunity to produce a broader variety of finishes.

The first firing is known as the **bisque** or **biscuit** fire. Depending upon the given maturity of the chosen clay, a bisque fire is heated within the cone 010 to cone 05 range (887° to 1031° C/1634 ° to 1841° F). During this fire all organic materials are burned away, chemically combined water is driven out and the composition of the clay is irreversibly changed. The sculpture is still porous enough to accept glaze.

At this low temperature the clay does not glassify, so it is safe to use support props without fear of them fusing to the sculpture. Make these props hollow and from the same clay — ideally at the same time as the form is being constructed. The props will shrink at the same rate as the form throughout the work cycle. During the fire they will continue to shrink accordingly and provide adequate support. After the bisque fire, when the form can stand on its own, discard the props.

Firing Sequence

Stack the kiln properly, check to see that the shelves are secure and place the proper cones in position. Although different kilns are fired in different ways, a basic bisque fire should proceed slowly. Start the kiln at a low setting with the door ajar or the spy holes open. This allows the atmospheric water to escape from the clay, the walls of the kiln and its furniture. After several hours, close the kiln and slowly increase the heat at a rate of about 50 degrees an hour until the chemically combined water has been driven from the clay — around 450° to 600° C (842° to 1112° F). Fire the kiln at a rate of about 100 degrees a hour until bisque temperature is reached. Do this by turning up switches at two hour intervals on electric kilns or slowly increasing air/fuel mixtures on fuel kilns.

A slower fire is a safer fire. The clay is less likely to shatter or crack if plenty of time is allowed for chemical changes to take place. As an electric kiln nears temperature it might be necessary to turn one or more switches down to equalize the heat throughout the kiln. Once temperature has been reached, shut off the kiln. Remember to tightly close dampers on a fuel kiln and to let the kiln cool slowly. The cooling cycle normally takes twice as long as the heating cycle.

GLAZE FIRING

Stack a glaze kiln the same way as a bisque kiln. Use clean kiln-washed shelves with proper three-point support. Place cones so that they can be easily seen. The main difference is that no two pieces, props included, should be allowed to touch. During the fire, glaze melts and will fuse with anything it touches. Check to see that works have no glaze on the bottom and that they are placed a safe distance from other works, as well as kiln furniture and walls. If a piece must be completely glazed, use only the best quality stilts rated for that particular temperature. Be certain that the form rests securely on the stilts.

Because the clay has already been bisque fired, the early stages of glaze firing can proceed more rapidly. A temperature rise of about 100 degrees an hour is reasonable. After red heat, glazes begin to go through certain chemical changes. As the glazes near maturity, slow the temperature rise to allow volatile materials to escape and the glazes to bubble and then smooth out. When the guide cone starts to bend, watch the kiln more carefully. When the desired temperature has been reached, slow the fire just enough to maintain that temperature for at least a half-hour. This **soaking period** allows the temperature to become even throughout the kiln and insures complete melting of the glazes.

Shut off the kiln, close dampers tightly and cool the kiln very slowly. On some kilns, pilot lights or low heat settings might be used to keep them from cooling too rapidly. The clay and glazes need time contract and stiffen. Otherwise, glazes could craze or pinhole and clay could crack or split. Fast firing is not recommended because the clay might shatter or split and glaze flaws like crawling or underfiring could occur.

REDUCTION FIRING

There are two major types of firing, each named for the atmospheric conditions inside the kiln. An **oxidation** firing is progressing well when the air/fuel mixture is such that a bright, clear kiln atmosphere occurs as when firing a bisque. **Reduction** in a fuel kiln can be achieved by increasing the fuel or decreasing the air. This creates a murky, slightly smoky atmosphere which reduces the amount of available oxygen in the kiln, hence the name. Electric kilns are said to fire in oxidation. In truth, because there is no actual combustion, the kilns fire in a **neutral** atmosphere.

Oxidation firings offer the brightest glaze colors, enhance under- and overglaze effects, and provide generally consistent results. A reduction fire brings out subtle color variations in both clay and glazes and often gives unique and unexpected results.

It is not wise to attempt reduction firing in an electric kiln. While several methods may impart a reduction look to fired ware, kiln elements are also affected and are more likely to suffer early failure.

When firing reduction in a fuel kiln, it is more efficient to have the initial stages heat in oxidation with a clear, bright flame. At about cone 017 (727° C/1341° F) bring the kiln to reduction to affect the clay body. To go from oxidation to reduction, change the air/fuel mixture until flames begin licking from the spy holes. Close the damper until slight back pressure is also evident in the flames. Keep the kiln in this light to medium reduction until the final cone is reached. Closing the damper too much can choke the kiln and actually cause the tem-

Jerry L. Caplan, *Tank Teapot*, 1987.
Clay, nails, 10″ (25.4 cm) tall.

perature to drop. Heavy reduction not only wastes fuel and pollutes the atmosphere, but can cause ware to bloat and glazes to pinhole.

As the temperature increases, flames will begin to show through the damper and spyholes. Keep a red-yellow tint to the flame in early firing stages. As the cycle progresses, the flame should become green to blue. If the flame is bright orange with black smoke, reduction is too heavy. Only a small amount of carbon monoxide is necessary to affect the oxides in the glazes. Heavy reduction merely deposits unburned carbon on the ware, clouding the finished colors.

When the final cone is almost fully bent, hold the temperature and atmosphere and soak for about 30 minutes to insure full development of the reduction glazes. At the end of the firing, turn the kiln to oxidation for 1 or 2 minutes to "clear the kiln." This can brighten copper reds and lessen the possibility of surface scum on glazes.

No matter what temperature or atmosphere, cool all kilns slowly to diminish the chances of fired ware **dunting** and glazes from crazing.

12 COMMISSIONS

A 15th century papal commission.
Gianlorenzo Bernini. *Ecstasy of Saint Theresa.*
Marble (3.5 m) tall.
Location: Cornaro Chapel. Santa Maria della Vittoria, Rome.

Bernini, Cellini and Buonarroti all had grand visions for massive sculptures, fountains and walls. Today, artists still have similar majestic ideas. However, it is one thing to have such dreams and quite another to have the wherewithal to produce these monumental projects.

One approach toward achieving this goal is by securing a commission. A commission is a very different way of producing art. Many artists do not feel comfortable creating works which frequently must include the wishes of others, often along with an apparently unreasonable legal requirement or two. If such restrictions can be considered acceptable, a commission can often provide for work of a greater scale, afford recognition for the artist (as well as increased compensation) and, occasionally, the opportunity to stretch one's artistic wings.

In earlier times, the usual way of securing a commission was by being contacted by a private donor who would bankroll the project. Once in a while a commission would come from some institution or government office. More recently, it has become necessary for the artist to actively solicit funding for any projects envisioned.

One good way to find out what nearby projects are in the works is to contact local arts associations. They usually have a listing of individuals, groups or organizations seeking artworks for special programs.

States with "percent for art" programs must, by law, set aside a certain percentage (usually ½ to 1 percent) of the cost of any new public construction to incorporate works of art. The state arts council should be ready to provide the necessary information. On a national level, the General Services Administration acts as a clearing house for all federal building projects.

Many national arts and architecture magazines and newsletters include information about current or pending architectural projects. Of course, newspapers, magazines, radio and television items can also provide leads about possible opportunities.

PLACES TO LOOK

Aside from the route of exhibitions and gallery showings, a productive way to have work accessible to others is by being represented in slide banks. Many local arts councils have slide banks with several examples of each member artist's work available for viewing. Many state agencies, including those for arts, education and transportation, often have similar arrangements. They keep examples of artists' work on file for viewing each time a new construction proposal is unveiled. There are also several good national slide banks. The federal General Services

PLACES TO BE FOUND

Sculpture at U.S. Port of Entry,
San Luis, Arizona.
Maria Alquilar. *Bien Venida y Vaya Con Dios*,
© 1987. Glazed stoneware, underglazes, china
paint. Metal fabrication by Joe Y. Kim,
15 x 6½ x 9½' (4.6 x 2 x 2.9 m).
Paid for by a grant from the General Services
Administration, Art in Architecture Program.

Administration has a computerized registry of artists. The Veterans
Administration has a similar program for buildings under its jurisdic-
tion. The privately funded International Sculpture Center in Washington, D.C., also has a computerized listing and referral service. A few
commercial slide banks are also in operation. For a fee, they will show
examples of an artist's work to interested parties.

For best exposure, it would be expedient to have examples of work
on file in several different places. Slides and backup materials, such as
articles and reviews, should be periodically updated. Do not depend on
the agency to send reminders.

Even with all of the foregoing bases covered, the best chance of getting a commission is often by word of mouth.

SLIDES

It is essential that works be shown to their best advantage. Use only
professional quality, original color slides. Present full view and detail

pictures taken from several angles. If the work is site specific, try to include slides showing views before and after installation. Otherwise, photograph the work against a plain background — minus studio tools, shrubbery, and the family car.

When the possibility of securing a commission is imminent, several steps are necessary to insure success.

The basis for finalizing a contract is in clearly articulating the concept for the client in the fullest manner possible. In many cases clients may state specific desires. After careful discussion, the artist may discover that clients do not know what they really want. To avoid later

STARTING OFF

Commission for a private residence. Paula Winokur, *Fireplace Site III,* 1985. Porcelain, metallic sulfates, ceramic pencil, 55 x 50 x 13″ (139.7 x 127 x 33 cm). Courtesy: Helen Drutt Gallery, New York and Philadelphia. Photograph: Will Brown.

conflicts it is wise to fully discuss the project options, gently steering the client toward a reasonable goal.

The essence of a commission is compromise. A creative artist can often bring fresh ideas to a client and develop a more exciting concept than was originally imagined. It must be remembered however, that the artist rarely has total control over the outcome. Client wishes, fiscal restraints and practical considerations often mitigate the actual product. The ultimate goal is not always the "look" of the work, but the fact that artist and client can find the results pleasing and livable and even feel good that a worthwhile contribution to society has been created.

WHERE TO START

First, face to face discussions with the client along with a visit to the site are in order. If for some reason this is not possible, request the most complete documentation available: photos of the site, plans, blueprints — including all necessary dimensions and the client's wish list.

Ask about local building code restrictions relative to the specific project. It is best to know these before work gets too far along. Size restrictions, weight limitations, regulations regarding the use of certain materials and approved installation methods are among the things to be researched. Keep good notes.

IDEA SKETCHES

Armed with this information, the next step is to develop a series of personal idea sketches — on paper or in three dimensions, whichever seems appropriate — to develop the forms, solidify the aesthetics and evolve the total concept toward the desired goal.

During this development stage, keep in mind such things as the following.

• How the site is normally used.

• Who uses the site.

• What the existing site contains, both visually and emotionally. Can any of this be retained, eliminated or enhanced.

Maquette for larger work by Jeanette Lazebnik Bernhard.

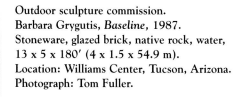

Outdoor sculpture commission.
Barbara Grygutis, *Baseline*, 1987.
Stoneware, glazed brick, native rock, water,
13 x 5 x 180′ (4 x 1.5 x 54.9 m).
Location: Williams Center, Tucson, Arizona.
Photograph: Tom Fuller.

• Are particular values associated with the site and can they be symbolized.

• Is the environment homogeneous or made of disparate elements.

• How will this new work relate to all of these concerns.

Practical and technical considerations can often affect the aesthetic outcome. It is better to have potential problems resolved before presenting the proposal to a client. While there is often more "wiggle room" when dealing with a private client, public commissions usually have more stringent rules and regulations which must be met.

PUBLIC PROJECTS

Publicly funded projects are usually announced on a competition basis. A prospectus is available to applicants which states the scope of the proposed project, including financing, due dates for proposals, the mechanics of choosing finalists and other pertinent information.

Most competitions require applicants to submit examples of previous works and résumés along with written proposals. Sometimes drawings or three-dimensional scale models of the artist's concept are requested. The more affluent competitions usually offer compensation to artists chosen to submit such models.

PRESENTATION

Institutional and public projects usually require some type of formal presentation of the artist's concept. Although this may not be necessary for a private commission, such a presentation is always good practice.

The more information that can be shown to the client at the outset, the less confusion and discord will arise later.

A possible presentation might consist of the following.

1. Projected slides or enlarged photos of the site as it currently appears.

2. A picture of the proposed work superimposed on the site photo.

3. Scale drawings (in color, if needed) showing several views.

Presentation model for possible commission.

Completed installation of commissioned
wall piece.
Carol Olbum, *Horizon*, 1986.
Stoneware, underglazes, glaze stains,
13 x 3′ x 4″ (4 x .9 m x 10.2 cm).
Installed: Lobby, Regional State Office
Building, Green Bay, Wisconsin.
Photograph: Bob Wertel.

4. A three-dimensional scale model large enough to be easily understood.

5. Full-sized samples in the final material to show color, texture and detail work.

6. A proposed time and compensation schedule.

7. Any additional information regarding use, safety, maintenance and other pertinent facts.

Calculating financial remuneration for commission work is somewhat different than works produced for artistic expression or the love of art. Costs must be figured accurately *before* the work commences, not after completion.

HOW MUCH?

PUBLIC COMMISSIONS

Many competitions and public commissions state a figure in the prospectus not to be exceeded. At first glance, the amount, with all its zeros, might seem to be more than adequate. A cost analysis can determine if this is indeed the case.

To arrive at the final cost of a work, several factors must be taken into account.

• **Preliminary work** including time and materials expense for all drawings, photography, model construction, necessary materials testing and possible legal research of building codes and permits.

• **Construction costs** or payment for the time it takes to model and build the actual work. An appropriate hourly wage must be figured for the artist and any helpers.

• **Materials costs** which cover actual expenses incurred for clay and glaze materials plus a percentage for handling and loss during construction.

• **Firing costs** for the time taken to load, fire and unload the kiln as well as the cost of fuel consumed.

• **Installation cost** or payment for the artist and others involved with placing the finished work on the site. Expenses for materials used for proper installation are to be included.

• **Overhead** consists of studio heat, light, rent, telephone use, insurance, travel and other studio related expenses.

• **Miscellaneous** expenses are any outlays related directly to the particular project which are not mentioned in the list above.

It may also be the case that *outside help* will be needed such as transportation, riggers, excavation and laborers. These costs must be established beforehand and also included in the estimate.

On major projects, the question of who will carry *liability insurance* during the construction phase and who should assume liability after installation must be worked out as well. Sometimes the artist must carry the policy during construction, even if there is a general contractor.

A commission for a public institution.
Author, *The Blackstone Canal in 1830*, 1988.
Matt glazed porcelain, lusters, 4 x 8′ (1.2 x 2.4 m).
Installed: Worcester Historical Museum, Worcester,
Massachusetts. Photograph: the author.

The Blackstone Canal in 1830 (detail).

The Blackstone Canal in 1830.
(Detail showing extent of relief.)

Usually the responsibility shifts to the client after the installation is completed.

The total of these figures is just the cost of the project. A suitable *profit* must also be included in the final estimate. Otherwise, the artist will have worked for free. Generally a profit margin of 10 to 15 percent of the total project is considered reasonable.

PRIVATE COMMISSIONS

Sometimes there is more leeway with a private or institutional commission. Once in a while the artist is given the opportunity to propose a work without a predetermined payment. Again, at first glance this might seem worthwhile, but try to establish a price range if possible. Prepare cost estimates as described, but in this case prepare two proposals: two versions of the project. In this way, if the primary proposal is questioned because of cost, rather than scaling it down to fit the budget and reducing or losing its aesthetic appeal — the second simplified, but equally stimulating, proposal can be introduced. However, in the author's experience, after appropriate detailed discussions have taken place, the second proposal has never been needed.

Left: A commission for a private residence. Dennis Christopher Murphy, *Untitled.* Glazed stoneware, 72 x 12 x 6″ (182.9 x 30.5 x 15.2 cm). Below: A large public project. Gail Corcoran-Freundt, *The New Life Mural,* 1984. Glazed porcelain, 7 x 100′ (2.1 x 30.5 m). Installed: MARTA Lakewood Station, Atlanta, Georgia. Photograph: Gary Bogue.

After the proposal has been viewed, discussed and accepted by all parties concerned, it is time to write a contract to protect both artist and client.

In some cases a simple letter of agreement is all that is necessary. The letter should state that the artist will produce a particular work, as previously approved by the client, on or about a certain date for an established compensation from the client. Include any information such as acceptable minor variations of the finished work, payment schedule, work to be done by outside labor and other agreed upon provisions. Both parties then sign the letter. A witness may sign as well, but this is not always necessary. Then the work begins.

Larger, lengthier public or institutional projects may require more formal contracts. If these clients have prepared contracts it would be prudent to consult a lawyer to determine if the artist's interests are properly noted and protected before signing.

CONTRACTS

Stephen Knapp, Untitled, © 1988.
Ceramic tile, 9′ × 62′.
The Spa at the Heritage, Boston.

GLOSSARY OF CERAMIC TERMS AND RAW MATERIALS

absorption   The capacity of a material to soak up liquid.

adsorption   The collecting of liquid on a surface by condensation.

additive   The creation of a sculpture through the process of building and adding material.

alkalies   Base compounds of sodium, potassium and alkaline earths which function as low temperature fluxes for silica.

alumina (Al_2O_3)   Increases viscosity, refractoriness and opacity of a glaze. Improves glaze hardness and resistance to chemicals. Also increases heat resistance in clay bodies.

alumina hydrate ($Al_2O_3 \cdot 3H_2O$)   A compound used primarily in stacking and firing to prevent clay objects from sticking to kiln shelves.

amorphous   Without specific form.

antimony oxide (Sb_2O_3)   A compound used chiefly in combination with lead compounds to derive a yellow colorant. **This compound, Naples Yellow, is poisonous.**

appliqué   A decorating technique by which bits of clay are adhered directly to plastic clay.

armature   A framework around which clay can be modeled.

art haut   A French phrase meaning "high art."

asbestos   A fibrous hydrous-silicate material formerly used for insulation and fireproofing. **Inhalation of asbestos fibers can cause severe lung problems.**

baffle (bag wall)   A wall or barrier made of refractory material which directs the flow of heat and flame in a fuel kiln.

banding wheel   See "bench wheel."

barium carbonate ($BaO \cdot CO_2$)   The primary source of barium oxide used to induce mattness in a glaze. A moderately active flux around cone 6 (1201° C/2194° F) and higher. Also used to prevent efflorescence in earthenware clay bodies.

barium oxide (BaO)   A moderately active flux at high temperatures. In high amounts it can produce mattness in a glaze. **In their raw state, barium compounds can be poisonous.**

barrier cream   A cream applied to skin to act as a protective shield.

bas relief (low-relief)   Raised or indented sculptural patterns which remain close to the surface plane.

bat   A disk or slab of plaster or other material used for drying clay or supporting clay forms while being worked.

batch   The ingredients of a glaze formula weighed in correct proportions for a specific blend.

bench wheel   A portable turntable for rotating clay objects while being formed, decorated or otherwise worked.

bentonite ($Al_2O_3 \cdot 4SiO_2 \cdot 9H_2O$)   A clay of volcanic origin used as a plasticizer in clay and also as a floatative in glaze.

binder   A material added prior to firing to increase glaze adherence or greenware strength.

bisque or **bisquit**   Clay which has been fired once, unglazed.

bisque fire   The first firing of a clay. This fire drives out chemically combined water and carbonaceous materials prior to glazing.

blistering   Air bubbles appearing in a glaze after fast firing.

block and case   Plaster molds used to make production molds.

blowout   The explosion of clay in a kiln caused by sudden escape of steam resulting from rapid heating or the presence of impurities.

bone ash ($13CaO \cdot 4P_2O_5 \cdot CO_2$)   Ground up calcined animal bones, used as a flux and minor opacifier in low temperature glazes. **Irritant.**

bone dry   The condition of unfired clay that has no absorbed moisture other than natural humidity.

borax ($Na_2O \cdot 2B_2O_3 \cdot 1OH_2O$)   Second to lead, the chief flux for low temperature glazes. It brings about bright colors, reduces viscosity and heals application defects. Borax, however, is soluble in water. **Can cause nasal and skin irritation.**

boric acid ($B_2O_3 \cdot 3H_2O$)   A soluble compound sometimes introduced into a glaze when the sodium content of borax is not desired.

boric oxide (B_2O_3)   A compound that helps reduce glaze expansion and reduces crazing. Can induce mottled colors and opalescence.

b.t.u.   British thermal unit. The amount of heat needed to raise one pound of water by one degree Fahrenheit.

burnish   The use of a smooth object to polish the surface of leather-hard clay.

calcine   To heat to the temperature necessary to drive off chemically combined water, carbon dioxide and other volatile gases.

calcium chloride ($CaCl_2$)   A compound used to thicken glaze slip.

calcium carbonate or **whiting** ($CaO \cdot CO_2$)   The chief source of calcium oxide for glazing.

calcium oxide (CaO)   A high temperature flux. Will bring about a melt at low temperatures when combined with other fluxes. Calcium oxide makes glazes harder, more durable, less soluble and lowers expansion rates.

calorie   A metric unit of heat. The amount of heat necessary to raise one gram of water one degree Celsius.

carving   Decorating by cutting into the clay surface.

castable   A mixture of sand, cement and refractory materials used to make kiln walls and kiln furniture.

casting or **slip casting**   A process of forming a clay object by pouring clay slip into a hollow plaster mold.

catenary arch   A type of kiln shape determined by the curve of a chain with its ends suspended the floor width apart and as high as the kiln is to be tall.

chemically combined water   The water chemically bound to alumina and silica in clay molecules.

china   Whiteware clay bodies glazed at a lower temperature than the temperature at which they are bisqued.

china clay   See "kaolin." A white firing, highly refractory primary clay.

chrome oxide (Cr_2O_3)   A compound used primarily as a green colorant. **Skin irritant. Inhalation can cause lung damage. Ingestion can be fatal.**

clay   A compound of decomposed and altered feldspathic rock consisting of various hydrated silicates of aluminum along with nonplastics, such as quartz, and organic matter. It is also used as a source of alumina and silica in glazes. **Long term exposure to clay dusts can cause lung disease.**

cobalt carbonate ($CoO•CO_2$)   A blue colorant reliable at all temperatures and both firing atmospheres.

cobalt oxide (CoO)   A considerably stronger version of blue colorant. Approximately one-half the amount is needed to produce colors similar to the carbonate. **May cause allergic reaction.**

coil   Rope-like roll of clay used in hand building.

colemanite or **gerstley borate** ($2CaO•3B_2O_3•5H_2O$) The only source of boric oxide that is insoluble except for commercial frits. Used as a low temperature flux. At higher temperatures it gives an opalescent quality to glazes. **Can be corrosive to skin.**

cone or **pyrometric cone**   A small elongated triangular pyramid made of ceramic materials which are compounded to bend and melt at a specific temperature. The cone serves as a time-temperature indicator of heat work in a kiln.

copper carbonate ($CuO•CO_2$)   Major green colorant in oxidation. In reduction, can give red colors. **Fumes released during firing can be toxic.**

copper oxide (CuO)   Green colorant in oxidation, can give red colors in reduction. One and one-half times more available copper than the carbonate. Above cone 8 (1236° C/2257° F) copper becomes volatile and can affect nearby glazes. **Fumes can be toxic.**

cornwall stone   A natural mineral containing feldspar, flint, clay and other materials. Primarily used as a flux. It can help reduce glaze shrinkage in unfired and fired state. **May contain fluorides which when fired release toxic fluorine gas.**

cottle or **coddle**   Any smooth flexible material, such as vinyl or galvanized sheet metal, used in moldmaking to contain plaster.

crackle glaze   A glaze developing minute cracks considered decorative. Often accentuated with rubbed-in coloring material.

crawling   Separation of glaze coating during firing, leaving exposed areas of clay.

crazing   The undesirable formation of a network of cracks in a glaze caused by uneven clay or glaze contraction.

cryolite ($3NaF•AlF_3$)   A violent flux at higher temperatures, causing pinholes and blisters. With proper temperature control, cryolite can give colorations similar to alkaline fluxes but with interesting striations. **Fluorine gas released during firing can be toxic.**

crystalline glaze   Characterized by macrocrystal clusters embedded in opaque glaze.

damper   A device used to adjust the draft in a fuel kiln by opening or closing the flue.

de-air   To remove air from clay.

decal   A transfer print applied onto glaze fired objects and fired at low temperature.

deflocculant   A substance used to bring about better suspension of a material in a liquid by neutralizing the electronic charge of its particles.

deflocculate   To evenly disperse particles throughout a liquid.

della robbia ware   Ceramic sculpture or relief plaques of glazed terra-cotta, produced in Florence by the family of Lucca della Robbia during the fifteenth century.

devitrification   The loss of gloss due to recrystallization of a glaze during cooling.

dipping   Coating ceramic objects by immersing them in slip or glaze.

dolomite ($CaO•MgO•2CO_2$)   A natural mineral containing calcium oxide and magnesium oxide. An effective flux at higher temperatures and at lower temperatures when combined with other fluxes. Dolomite will assist in forming a smooth buttery glaze surface and can also be used to increase firing range in a clay body.

draw trials   Samples taken from a kiln during firing to check progress.

dry foot   The bottom of a ceramic object which has been cleaned of all glaze before firing.

downdraft   A type of kiln with the firebox and chimney at opposite ends from each other at or below the floor.

dunting   Cracking of fired ware in a kiln which has cooled too rapidly.

earthenware   Clay that matures at a low temperature but remains porous.

efflorescence   Dry or crystallized white scum on the surface of fired clay caused by unneutralized soluble salts.

egyptian paste   Low-fire, self-glazing porous clay developed in ancient Egypt.

elephant ear sponge   A natural sponge so named because of its shape.

elements   High resistance wire coils or bars used as the heat source in electric kilns.

engobe   A slurry of glaze materials used to decorate dry or bisqued clay.

excise   To carve away the background around a decoration, leaving the image in raised relief.

extrusion   The process of making shapes by forcing clay through a die.

feldspar (KNaO)   The principal flux in most high temperature glazes. Natural mineral containing alkalines, alumina and silica. There are three common forms of feldspar: soda, calcium and potash.

fettle or **fettling**   To trim the excess clay from cast ware.

filler   A material with little or no plasticity used to promote drying and reduce shrinkage in clay bodies.

filter press   A machine which removes excess water from clay slip by pressure to make plastic clay.

firebox   The combustion chamber of a gas, oil or wood-fired kiln directly below or beside the ware chamber.

firebrick   A refractory insulation brick.

fireclay   A clay used in clay bodies for its heat-resistant qualities. Also used in the manufacture of kilns and other refractory equipment.

firing   The heating of clay or glaze to a specific temperature.

fit   The correct adjustment of a glaze to a clay body.

flaking   The peeling off of a glaze or slip from a clay surface.

flashing   a. Excess clay on an object left by the seam lines of a mold. b. The resultant color change on clay or glaze left by direct flame during a fuel firing.

flint or **quartz** (SiO_2)   The main source of silica for glazing. Adding flint to a glaze decreases its thermal expansion. Added to a clay body, it increases thermal expansion, reduces dry and fired shrinkage and increases refractoriness. **Continued inhalation over time can cause silicosis, which may lead to serious lung damage.**

flocculate   To cause the aggregation of clay particles.

flocking   Powdered felt used as decorating material.

flue   The space around the ware chamber of a kiln through which heating gases pass from the firebox to chimney.

fluorspar or **calcium fluoride** (CaF_2)   An opacifier and flux in the glass industry. Somewhat limited use as glaze flux. **Fluorine gas released during firing can be toxic.**

flux   A substance which promotes the melting of silica in a glaze.

foot   The base of a ceramic piece.

frit   A glass-like fusion of ceramic materials similar in composition to feldspar. Reground frits are used to introduce water-soluble, toxic, or otherwise difficult materials into a glaze in a prefired state.

glaze   A glass-like coating, fusion bonded to a ceramic surface by heat.

glaze fire   A cycle during which glaze materials are heated sufficiently to melt, forming a glassy surface coating when cooled.

glitter   Metallic colored plastic flakes used for decoration.

gold (Au)   Fired metallic overglaze decoration available as liquid bright gold, powder or paste gold, or liquid burnished gold.

greenware   Unfired clay objects.

grog   Fired clay that has been crushed into granules which may be added to a clay body to increase strength, control drying and reduce shrinkage.

grout   Mortar or similar compounds used to consolidate objects by filling spaces between them.

gum   A natural gum, such as gum arabic or gum tragacanth, used as a binder in glaze to promote better adherence to clay. Veegum T and Veegum CER are manufactured compounds for similar use.

hard paste   A hard, white, translucent clay body fired to cone 12 or above; a true porcelain.

high relief   A strongly raised or deeply carved pattern.

hydrometer   An instrument for determining the specific gravity of a liquid.

ilmenite ($TiO_2 \cdot FeO$)   A high iron mineral containing titanium. In powdered form, will opacify and darken a glaze. Granular ilmenite produces speckles in a glaze or clay body.

impressing   Method of decorating by stamping into a plastic clay surface.

incising   Engraving a decoration into unfired clay.

iron chromate ($FeO \cdot CrO_3$)   A compound used to produce brown colors in underglazes and glazes. Can also be used to darken clay bodies. **Can cause skin irritation. Inhalation can cause lung damage.**

iron oxide   Commonly used in two forms: **Ferric oxide** (Fe_2O_3) known as red iron oxide, can be used as a brown colorant in both clay bodies and glazes. A fine powder that easily stains everything it contacts. **Ferrous oxide** (FeO), known as black iron oxide, is a coarse form of powdered iron. Nonstaining, ferrous oxide can be substituted for red iron oxide in smaller amounts because of its greater iron/oxygen ratio. It tends, however, to give slightly mottled effects.

kanthal   A high resistance metal alloy used to manufacture heating elements for electric kilns.

kaolin   See "china clay." The anglicized form of the Chinese term for clay. Kao-Lin, meaning "high hill," probably refers to Kaoling, the mountain in China where this white clay was first discovered.

keys   Matching bumps and depressions used to correctly align sections of a plaster mold.

kiln   A furnace or oven for calcining or firing ceramic products.

kiln furniture   Refractory shelves, posts and other equipment placed in a kiln to hold ware during firing.

kiln wash   A refractory mixture, usually of kaolin and flint, applied to kiln shelves and floor to prevent fired glaze from adhering.

kneading   Working clay on a surface with the palms of the hands to remove air and obtain uniform consistency.

A NOTE ABOUT LEAD

Lead is an all pervading natural element. An average of 16 parts per million (ppm) of lead is in the earth's crust and is found in soil the world over. Small quantities of lead are therefore unavoidably present in food and water. Industrial processes, auto exhaust and waste disposal emit thousands of tons of lead into the air each year. Although small doses of lead may slowly pass from the body, larger amounts remain, usually in the bones. Eventually this can cause lead intoxication, permanent damage to brain or bones, even death. Currently, 15 to 20 ppm of lead in the bloodstream is accepted as the average adult accumulation. Forty ppm is considered dangerous. A simple blood test can indicate the amount of lead in the blood. Chemical therapy is available to reduce, if not totally eliminate, the amount of lead in the body.

For centuries lead has been a primary flux in glass and glaze. Its desirable properties of low fusability, brilliance, luster and smoothness are not easily equalled by other fluxes. Properly fritted with other glaze materials into lead silicate or other forms, lead becomes virtually insoluble and safer to use in glazing. Firing a leaded glaze to the proper temperature for which it is compounded will also help reduce the possibility of "free" lead remaining in the glaze or on its surface.

When using lead compounds in the studio, be certain there is adequate ventilation. Wear rubber gloves and an approved respirator mask. Fire lead glazes with proper ventilation. Follow these procedures when working with silica, barium, copper, cobalt or any other toxic substance.

A simple method of avoiding lead contamination in a glaze is not to use lead. Lead volatilizes and is no longer a usable flux above cone 6 (1201° C/2194° F).

lead carbonate or **white lead** ($3PbO \cdot 2CO_2 \cdot H_2O$) A low temperature flux. Its relative purity, small particle size and ready fusability make it the most reasonable way to introduce lead into a glaze. **Over a period of time, inhalation of dry powder can cause lead poisoning.**

lead oxide Two forms of lead oxide are used in ceramics: **litharge** (PbO); and **red lead** (Pb_3O_4). Litharge, or yellow lead, has a coarser particle size and is less effective than red lead. Red lead is less expensive than white lead, but stains everything it contacts. Because of its higher lead content, it is used in frit preparation. **Toxic.**

leather-hard The condition of raw clay when most of the moisture has evaporated, but is still soft enough to be carved or joined to other pieces.

lithium carbonate ($Li_2 \cdot CO_2$) A source of lithium for fluxing high temperature glaze. Lithium carbonate gives the glaze a high gloss and bright color response and can also be used in mid-range glazes in place of lead. **In water, can be a skin irritant. Ingested, it can damage bone marrow.**

LOI Loss on ignition. The amount of materials burned away during firing.

luster A type of metallic decoration applied to a fired glazed surface and refired to a temperature just high enough to fuse the metal to the glaze.

luting Joining leather-hard or dry clay with slip or vinegar.

macaloid A refined naturally occurring material which can be used as a plasticizer in clay bodies.

magnesium carbonate ($MgO \cdot CO_2$) A compound that makes low temperature glazes matt and opaque. It acts as a flux in high temperature glazes, giving smooth buttery surface. Cobalt blues turn purple or pinkish in high magnesium glazes. **Fumes can be toxic.**

magnesium sulfate or **epsom salts** ($MgO \cdot SO_3 \cdot 7H_2O$) A compound used to help prevent glaze from settling. A tablespoon per thousand grams is usually sufficient.

manganese carbonate ($MnO \cdot CO_2$) A compound used as a colorant in mid-temperature glazes to give blue-purple to plum colors. Above cone 6 colors tend toward brown. **Irritant.**

manganese dioxide (MnO_2) A compound that acts in a manner similar to manganese carbonate. Because it is coarse grained, it tends to make dark specks and is therefore also used in clay bodies. **Inhalation of fumes can permanently damage nervous system.**

maquette   French term for three-dimensional model or study for a larger work.

matt   The nonglossy surface quality of a completely fired glaze.

maturity   The firing point at which glaze ingredients have reached complete fusion or when clay has reached maximum nonporosity and hardness.

modeled-on   See "sprig."

mold   A plaster or bisqued clay shape from which a clay form can be reproduced.

molochite   White porcelain grog.

muffle   The inner lining of a fuel kiln which prevents flame from directly touching the ware.

muller   A grinding machine with rollers used to prepare large batches of clay.

neat cement   A mixture of calcined clay and limestone, without sand or other aggregate, used as a bonding agent.

nepheline syenite   A naturally occurring rock with characteristics similar to a high soda feldspar. It has a lower melting point than many spars and is therefore a good flux for mid-temperature glazes as well as at high temperatures.

neutral atmosphere   The atmosphere in a kiln between reduction and oxidation. This is only theoretically possible in a fuel kiln. It is possible, however, in an electric kiln because there is no flame.

nickel carbonate ($NiO \cdot CO_2$)   A weak form of nickel oxide colorant. **Irritant.**

nickel oxide (black: Ni_2O_3); (green: NiO)   A compound that gives grey to brown colors in glaze. In barium-calcium glazes may give purple to pink. **Irritant. Excessive inhalation could cause lung cancer.**

ochre   The name for a number of iron bearing surface clays which can be used as glaze or slip colorants. Fired colors range from tan to black.

once fire or **single fire**   A slow firing cycle which combines both bisque and glaze firings.

open   Refers to a clay body that is porous in structure because of grain size, fillers or grog.

open firing   A fuel firing in which the flame touches the ware directly.

opacifier   A relatively insoluble glaze substance. Minute particles reflect light and render the glaze opaque.

overglaze   A glaze decoration applied on the surface of a fired glaze which is then refired.

oxide   A compound containing oxygen and other elements. Sometimes refers to metallic chemicals used for coloring clays or glazes.

oxidation fire   A firing during which the kiln chamber retains an ample supply of oxygen.

parting line   In mold-making, the line drawn on the model accurately marking the division between mold sections.

pâte-sur-pâte   A decorating method consisting of built-up layers of engobe. From the French meaning "paste on paste."

pearl ash or **potassium carbonate** ($K_2O \cdot CO_2$)   A compound used as a potassium source for frits. Although soluble, may be used to alter colors produced by other colorants.

peeling   Separation of the fired glaze or slip from a clay surface because the clay has contracted more than the glaze.

petalite ($Li_2O \cdot Al_2O_3 \cdot 8SiO_2$)   A source for lithia and silica in mid- or high-temperature glazes. Effective flux for once-fired glazes. In a clay body, offers nearly zero expansion and excellent heat shock resistance.

piercing   Decorative cuts through a clay form.

pinch forming   A method of forming objects by pinching the clay wall with the fingers.

pinholing   Glaze flaw consisting of tiny holes caused by poor clay preparation, improper glaze application or incorrect firing.

pins   Refractory supports used to place ware in racks or saggars for firing.

pin tool   A needle-like tool used to trim uneven tops of wheel thrown clay objects.

plaster (gypsum)   Calcined hydrated calcium sulfate used in ceramics to make molds or bats.

plasticity   The quality of clay that allows it to be easily manipulated and still maintain its shape.

plastic vitrox   A mineral similar in activity to potash spar or cornwall stone. Source of silica, potash and alumina in a glaze.

platinum (Pt)   An element used as liquid bright platinum. It gives a fired overglaze luster color brighter than silver and less apt to tarnish.

porcelain   A strong, vitreous, translucent white clay body that matures at cone 12 or above.

porosity   The capacity of a fired clay body to absorb moisture.

pot lifters   Tools (usually metal) used to aid in the removal of freshly-thrown ware from the potter's wheel.

pressing   Forming objects by squeezing soft clay between two halves of a mold. Also, a method using fingers to impress a decoration into soft clay.

primary clay or **residual clay**   Clay found at the original site where it was formed by decomposing rock.

pug   To mix clay with water to make it plastic.

pug mill   A machine with a paddle gear for grinding and mixing plastic clay.

pyrometer   A bimetallic strip which translates heat energy into electrical energy, used to indicate the temperature in a kiln. Optical pyrometers perform the same function, but use color as the indicator.

pyrometric cone   See "cone."

pyrophyllite ($Al_2O_3 \cdot 4SiO_2 \cdot H_2O$)   A compound that decreases cracking, shrinking and warping in a ceramic body while increasing its firing range.

raku   The technique of rapidly firing low temperature glazed bisque ware. A Japanese symbol, raku means "enjoyment of leisure" or "contentment." This method is used to make bowls for tea ceremony.

raw   Unfired, in a natural state.

red heat   The firing temperature at which the interior of a kiln begins to glow.

reduction fire   A firing in which the supply of oxygen is inadequate to promote complete combustion. Carbon monoxide thus formed combines with oxygen in clay and glazes, altering their colors.

reductive   The method of creating a work by removing material.

refractory   The quality of resistance to high temperatures. Also, high alumina-silica material used in the manufacture of kiln furniture and interiors.

rib   A hand held tool made of hard material used to shape ceramic ware.

rutile (TiO_2)   An impure form of titanium oxide containing iron, chrome and vanadium. In powdered form, it is used as tan colorant or to opacify or mottle glaze. In granular form, it tends to give brown specks or streaks. Also used to color clay.

saggar or **sagger**   Fireclay box which protects ware from flame and combustion gases during a fuel firing.

sagging   The slumping of a form while plastic clay is still soft.

salt glaze   To glaze raw ware by vapors from common

salt introduced into a fuel kiln during firing. Also, the resultant glaze.

scaling   The flaking or peeling of a glaze.

scraping   The use of a serrated edge to decorate dry clay.

scratching   The use of a serrated edge to decorate plastic clay.

secondary clay or **sedimentary clay**   Clay that has been transported from its original site by water, air or ice and deposited in layers elsewhere.

sgraffito   A decorative process. A line is scratched through a layer of slip or glaze before firing to expose the clay underneath. From the Italian, meaning "scratched out."

shard or **sherd**   A fragment of fired pottery.

shims   Thin metal strips used to divide a model into workable sections when making multiple piece plaster molds.

short   Clay that is nonplastic and breaks or crumbles easily.

shrinkage   Contraction of clay or glaze in either drying or firing.

shrinking slab   A sheet of clay, made at the same time as a sculpture and placed under it to protect the base from distorting.

silica (SiO_2)   A compound that forms a hard glass when fired to its melting point. In glaze batches, it is added as a mineral combined in clay, spar or other materials. **Inhalation can cause silicosis and other lung problems.**

silica sand   A pure flint sand used as cushion between kiln shelf and object being fired. In small amounts, can be added to clay body to reduce shrinkage, warping and add texture.

silicon carbide (SiC)   A compound used in the manufacture of high temperature kiln shelves and other refractory parts. Finely ground particles introduced into a glaze can act as local reduction agent.

silver carbonate ($Ag_2O \cdot CO_2$)   A compound that becomes a metallic silver luster under light reduction at low temperature.

silver nitrate ($AgO \cdot NO_2$)   When mixed with resin and lavender oil and applied directly to a fired glaze surface this compound will give a silver-yellow metallic luster when fired in oxidation.

single fire   See "once fire."

sinter   To fire to the point where materials fuse sufficiently to form a solid mass upon cooling, but are not vitrified.

size or **sizing**   A solution used to prevent poured plaster from adhering to a surface.

slab   A flat sheet of clay.

slake   To pour dry material into a liquid and allow it to absorb the liquid to its fullest capacity.

slip   A suspension of clay or glaze materials in water.

slip clay   A clay containing sufficient flux to become a glaze when fired to high temperatures.

slip glaze   A glaze made chiefly from clay.

slurry   A creamy mixture of clay and water.

soak   To maintain the kiln at a particular temperature for a period of time.

soap   A brick cut in half lengthwise.

soda ash or **sodium carbonate** ($Na_2O \cdot CO_2$)   An active, but soluble flux usually added to a glaze in fritted form. Soda ash can be used as a deflocculant in slips and a suspender in engobes. It is also used as a glaze source for vapor glazing. **Corrosive to skin and eyes.**

soda firing   To glaze raw clay with vapors from soda ash or bicarbonate of soda introduced into fuel kiln during firing.

sodium bicarbonate or **bicarbonate of soda** ($N_2O \cdot H_2O \cdot 2CO_2$)   A compound used as a nonpoisonous alternative to sodium chloride for salt glazing. It acts as deflocculant in clay or glaze slips.

sodium chloride or **common salt** (NaCl)   A compound that vaporizes when introduced directly into a hot kiln, forming a glaze on exposed clay surfaces. This process is known as salt glazing. **Fumes can be toxic.**

sodium silicate or **water glass** ($Na_2O \cdot XSiO_2$)   A compound used as a clay slip deflocculant.

soft paste   A mixture of white firing clays and ground glass frit which matures about cone 05 (1031° C/1888° F).

soluble   Capable of being dissolved in liquid.

spall   To chip or splinter off.

spare   A plug of plaster or clay used to form the opening when making a slip-casting mold. Also, the opening itself. Spare sometimes refers to the excess clay to be trimmed from castware.

spodumene ($Li_2O \cdot Al_2O_3 \cdot 4SiO_2$)   A major source of lithium in glaze and clay bodies. Active flux at high temperatures. In some clay bodies can reduce shrinkage to zero.

sprig   A mold-made ornament of plastic clay applied to a clay surface to form a relief decoration.

sprung arch   A kiln with a slightly curving roof contained by a framework.

spur   A triangular refractory support which keeps glazed ware from touching kiln shelf during firing.

spy hole or **peep hole**   The opening in a kiln wall or door through which cones may be viewed during firing. It can also act as a steam vent during early stages of firing.

stacking   Efficient loading of a kiln with the maximum amount of ware.

stain   Prepared calcined pigment added to clay bodies or glazes for color. Also, a nonfired coloring agent for ceramic surfaces.

stamping   A method of decoration by pushing objects against plastic clay.

stilt   A ceramic tripod used to support glazed ware in a kiln during firing.

stoneware   Grey to buff colored, nontranslucent clay body which matures between cones 6 and 10.

stretching   The method by which a wheel thrown form is shaped from the inside.

strontium carbonate ($SrO \cdot CO_2$)   An active flux that can be used to replace lead in a glaze.

talc ($3MgO \cdot 4SiO_2 \cdot H_2O$)   A compound used in a glaze for both its magnesia and silica content. Mild flux and opacifier. Often used as a flux in low temperature clay bodies. **Inhalation can cause lung damage.**

temper   To allow time to age.

template   A pattern placed against a clay form as a guide in shaping.

terra-cotta   Brownish-orange earthenware clay body. From the Italian, meaning "baked earth."

terra sigillata   Originally referred to Roman stamped ware. The term has come to mean the thin slip coating as found on early Greek ware. Made of fine particles of decanted clay, it is thinly applied over a clay surface and then fired to a low temperature. From the Italian, meaning "stamped earth."

thixotropic   The property of becoming fluid or elastic when stirred or shaken. Can be induced in certain clays by excess deflocculation.

throw or **throwing**   To use the potter's wheel to make forms from plastic clay by hand.

throwing stick   A long-handled, spoon-shaped stick used for shaping interiors of tall narrow wheel-thrown forms.

tin chloride or **stannous chloride** (SnCl₂)   A widely used fuming agent in vapor glazing. It gives mother-of-pearl luster to glazed ware. **Wear a respirator when using. Fumes are toxic.**

tin oxide (SnO_2)   A most effective opacifier. One or two percent will opacify a glaze and improve its gloss. Five percent added to a glaze will completely opacify it.

titanium dioxide (TiO_2)   A compound used as an opacifier. A two or three percent addition can give a milky opalescence. Higher amounts can bring about mattness.

tooth   The quality of roughness in a clay caused by its coarse grain structure or the addition of grog or other fillers.

translucency   The ability to transmit diffused light.

trimming or **turning**   The method of paring away excess clay while the leather-hard form is rotating on the potter's wheel.

undercut   The inward slant of a mold which can prevent clay from being released.

underglaze   Colored decoration applied on raw or bisqued ware before the glaze is applied.

updraft   A type of kiln. The fuel is burned below the ware and the heat and gases exhaust above.

vanadium pentoxide (V_2O_5)   A compound used as a colorant to produce yellow to brown hues. Generally introduced into a glaze in the form of vanadium-tin stains which produce stronger yellows. **Inhalation can cause bronchitis.**

vapor glaze   To glaze raw ware by introducing soluble chemicals into a kiln during firing. See "salt glaze."

viscosity   The property of a liquid to resist movement.

vitreous   The hard, glassy and nonabsorbent quality of a clay body or glaze.

vitrify or **vitrification**   To fire to the temperature at which a clay or glaze attains its mature, hard, glass-like quality.

volatilize   To pass off as a vapor.

volcanic ash   Minute particles of volcanic glass. It can be used as a mid-range flux. In a low temperature clay body can produce less warping, greater strength and longer firing range. **Can cause irritation to skin and eyes.**

ware   Ceramic objects.

warping   Distortion of a clay form caused by uneven stresses during shaping, drying or firing.

wash   Coloring oxide mixed with water.

water smoking   Early stage of firing during which chemically combined water evaporates from the clay.

wax resist   Wax emulsion or melted wax used to prevent slip or glaze from adhering to a clay surface. It can also be used to retard the drying of leather-hard ware.

weathering   The exposure of raw clay to natural elements which break down particle size and render the clay more plastic.

wedge or **wedging**   Mixing and removing the air from plastic clay by cutting it diagonally and slamming the pieces together.

welding   Joining pieces of soft or leather-hard clay.

white lead   See "lead carbonate."

whiteware   Ware made from a white or light cream-colored clay body, usually fired to a low temperature.

whiting   See "calcium carbonate."

wollastonite (CaO•SiO_2)   Natural calcium silicate used as a glaze flux. It produces smoother, brighter glaze than whiting. Used in a clay body, it will reduce shrinkage, improve heat shock resistance and lower moisture expansion.

zinc oxide (ZnO) Glaze flux which improves gloss, reduces crazing, increases firing range and brightens colors. Large amounts can create mattness or cause crawling and pinholing. **Can cause skin irritation.**

zirconium oxide (ZrO₂) A compound used as an opacifier at all temperatures. Available as Zircopax, Superpax and others. Although less expensive than tin oxide, twice the material is needed to achieve the same opacity. **Can cause skin rash.**

page 92

BIBLIOGRAPHY

Barazani, Gail. *Ceramics Health Hazards: Occupational Safety and Health for Artists and Craftsmen,* revised. Boscobel, Wisconsin: Art-Safe, Inc., 1984, 20 p.

Brodie, Regis. *The Energy Efficient Potter.* New York: Watson-Guptill Publications, 1982, 206 p. illus.

Chaney, Charles and Skee, Stanley. *Plaster Mold and Model Making.* New York: Van Nostrand Reinhold Company, 1973, 144 p. illus.

Clark, Garth, ed. *Ceramic Art: Comment and Review 1882–1977.* New York: E. P. Dutton, 1978, 198 p. illus.

Frith, Donald E. *Mold Making for Ceramics.* Radnor, Pennsylvania: Chilton Book Company, 1985, 227. p. illus.

Hamilton, David. *Architectural Ceramics.* London: Thames and Hudson Ltd., 1978, 184 p. illus.

Janson, A. W. *History of Art,* revised and expanded by Anthony F. Janson. New York: Harry N. Abrams, Inc., 1986, 824 p. illus.

Langland, Tuck. *Practical Sculpture.* Englewood Cliffs, New Jersey: Prentice-Hall, 1988, 242 p. illus.

Nigrosh, Leon I. *Claywork: Form and Idea in Ceramic Design,* 2nd edition. Worcester, Massachusetts: Davis Publications, Inc., 1986, 256 p. illus.

———. *Low Fire: Other Ways to Work in Clay.* Worcester, Massachusetts: Davis Publications, Inc., 1980, 102 p. illus.

Olsen, Fredrick L. *The Kiln Book,* 2nd edition. Radnor, Pennsylvania: Chilton Book Company, 1983, 292 p. illus.

Preble, Duane and Sarah. *Art Forms,* 4th edition. New York: Harper & Row, Publishers, Inc., 1989, 516 p. illus.

Rawson, Philip. *Design.* Englewood Cliffs, New Jersey: Prentice-Hall, 1988, 352 p. illus.

Rhodes, Daniel. *Kilns: Design, Construction and Operation,* 2nd edition. Radnor, Pennsylvania: Chilton Book Company, 1980, 256 p. illus.

Williams, Arthur. *Sculpture: Technique, Form and Content.* Worcester, Massachusetts: Davis Publications, Inc., 1989, 360 p. illus.

PERIODICALS

American Craft (bimonthly)
40 West 53rd Street
New York, NY 10019

Ceramics Monthly (monthly)
Box 12448
Columbus, OH 43212

Sculpture (bimonthly)
1050 Potomac Street, NW
Washington, DC 20007

Anne Smith, *Teapot With Shelf,* 1987.
Wheel-thrown, reduction fired porcelain, wood, gouache, 12 x 12″ (30.5 x 30.5 cm).
Photograph: Dean Powell.

APPENDIX A
CLAY BODY AND GLAZE RECIPES

The following clay bodies and glaze recipes are offered by artists for those not satisfied with commercially available choices. Results may differ depending upon materials used. Always make and test sample batches before preparing any formulas in large quantity.

CLAY BODIES

Katherine L. Ross' Red Adobe

Cedar Heights Red Art	15
Fire Clay	15
Cement	30
Sand	25
1079 Dextrine	15
Improves surface hardness.	
	100

Susan and Steven Kemenyffy's Raku Body

Cedar Heights Gold Art	1/3
Fire Clay	1/3
Kyanite (35 mesh)	1/3

Harriet Brisson's Raku Body

Fire Clay	50
China Clay	15
Ball Clay	15
Grog	15
Talc	5
	100

E. E. Randall's C/04 Handbuilding Earthenware

Cedar Heights Red Art	20
Ocmulgee	30
Fire Clay	15
Talc	15
Wollastonite	10
Grog	10
	100

Bill Stewart's C/04 Terra-cotta

Cedar Heights Red Art	50
Ball Clay	40
Nepheline Syenite	10
	100
+ Barium Carbonate	1
+ Coarse Grog	25
+ Mullite (35 Mesh)	25

Robert Milne's C/02 Whiteware

Ball Clay	40
Talc	40
Fire Clay	20
	100

Debra Trager, *The Schoolroom.*
Pinchformed, slab-built, white stoneware, glaze stains, airbrushed glaze,
12 x 15 x 22" (30.5 x 38.1 x 55.9 cm).
Photograph: Ralph Gabriner.

Roberta Kaserman's C/1 Single-Fire Porcelain

China Clay	30
Ball Clay	20
Potash Feldspar	25
Flint	25
	100

Ann Holmes, *Neviads*.
Press molded, handbuilt stoneware.
Photograph: the artist.

**Katherine L. Ross' C/2 Reduction
Dark Brown**

Cedar Heights Red Art	50
Fire Clay	15
Stoneware Clay	15
Ball Clay	10
Blackbird Clay	10
	100
+ Red Iron Oxide	3
+ Grog	30

Valerie Bowe's C/G Stoneware

Cedar Heights Red Art	50
Ball Clay	50
Fire Clay	50
Grog (20/48 Mesh)	40

**Richard Shaw's C/8
Handbuilding Porcelain**

China Clay	35
Potash Feldspar	25
Flint	20
Ball Clay	10
Nepheline Syenite	10
	100

(Can be made into casting slip by
adding up to 1 percent of sodium
silicate, soda ash or other
deflocculant.)

**Tova Beck Freidman's
C/10 Stoneware**

Ball Clay	35
Fire Clay	40
Coarse Grog	10
Fine Grog	15
	100

**Harris Deller's C/10
Throwing Porcelain**

Grolleg	55
Potash Feldspar	13
Flint	20
Pyrophyllite	12
	100
+ Bentonite	2
+ Molochite (Fine)	7
+ Molochite (Coarse)	3

**Jeffrey Chapp's C/05-03 Whiteware
Casting Slip**

Ball Clay	30
China Clay	15
Talc	55
	100
+ Water	43
+ Deflocculant	2

**Francine Trearchis Ozereko,
Still Life With Flower Vase, 1988.**
Slab-built earthenware, underglazes,
glaze. 14 x 16 x 9″ (35.6 x 40.6 x
22.9 cm).
Photograph: U Mass Photo Service.

**Brian Buckley's C/9 Porcelain
Casting Slip**

Ball Clay	27
China Clay	27
Potash Feldspar	27
Flint	19
	100
+ Water	9 gallons
+ Sodium Silicate	4 ounces

Steffanie Samuels, *Waiting at the Gate*.
Wheel-thrown, constructed stoneware,
slips, glazes, 58 x 25 x 25″ (147.3 x
63.5 x 63.5 cm).
Photograph: R.H. Hensleigh.

GLAZES

Raku White Crackle

Gerstley Borate	80
China Clay	20
	100
+ Zircopax	10

C/04 Gloss

Colemanite NA	30
Ferro Frit 3124	30
China Clay	25
Flint	15
	100

C/4 Gloss

Soda Feldspar	44
Gerstley Borate	19
Dolomite	6
Whiting	2
Zinc Oxide	5
China Clay	5
Flint	19
	100

Jeune Nowak Wussow, *Country Children Dancing.*
Handbuilt reduction fired stoneware, 14″ (35.6 cm) tall.
Collection: Mrs. Bob Hope.
Photograph: Milwaukee Journal.

C/4 Matt

Potash Feldspar	51.6
Whiting	18.8
Zinc Oxide	8.6
China Clay	15.4
Flint	5.6
	100.0

C/6 Gloss

Nepheline Syenite	47
Gerstley Borate	27
China Clay	6
Flint	20
	100

C/6 Matt

Potash Feldspar	53.3
Whiting	10
Zinc Oxide	12
Barium Carbonate	20
Ball Clay	4.7
	100.0

Richard Shaw's C/8 Gloss

Whiting	21
China Clay	21
Flint	33
Potash Feldspar	12.5
Colemanite NA	12.5
	100

C/8 Matt

Potash Feldspar	37.8
Whiting	21.0
Cornwall Stone	16.8
China Clay	12.6
Zinc Oxide	10.1
Bentonite	1.7
	100.0

Warren Hullow/Isabel Parks' C/10 White Matt

Potash Feldspar	49
China Clay	25
Dolomite	22
Whiting	4
	100
+ Tin Oxide	6

Jerry L. Caplan, *Contact*, 1984.
Carved terra-cotta pipe.
6′ (1.8 m) tall.
Photograph: the artist.

Clay

Cedar Heights Clay Co.
Box 295
Oak Hill, OH 45656

A. P. Green Industries
Mexico, MO 65265

Hammill & Gillespie
Box 104
Livingston, NJ 07039

Minnesota Clay
8001 Grand Avenue South
Bloomington, MN 55420

Clay Mixers, Pug Mills

Bluebird Manufacturing Co.
Box 2307
Fort Collins, CO 80522

Peter Pugger
12501 Orr Springs Road
Ukiah, CA 95482

Shimpo
3500 West Devon Avenue
Lincolnwood, IL 60659

Soldner Pottery Equipment
Box 90
Aspen, CO 81612

Colorants, Stains

Mason Color & Chemical Works, Inc.
Box 76
East Liverpool, OH 43920

Decals

CeramiCorner
Box 516
Azusa, CA 91702

Wise Screenprint Inc.
1013 Valley Street
Dayton, OH 45404

Extruders, Slabrollers

Bailey Pottery Equipment Corp.
CPO 1577
Kingston, NY 12401

AMACO/Brent
4717 West 16th Street
Indianapolis, IN 46222

General Ceramic Supplies

AMACO
American Art Clay Co., Inc.
4717 West 16th Street
Indianapolis, IN 46222

A.R.T. Studio Clay Company
1555 Louis Avenue
Elk Grove Village, IL 60007

Bailey Pottery Equipment Corp.
CPO 1577
Kingston, NY 12401

Miami Clay Co.
270 NE 183 Street
Miami, FL 33179

**Karen Park, *Table Fountain*.
Slab-built, hand-formed stoneware, glaze,
78¾ x 78¾" (200 x 200 cm).**

Standard Ceramic Supply Co.
Box 4435
Pittsburgh, PA 15205

Trinity Ceramics
9016 Diplomacy Row
Dallas, TX 74247

Laguna Clay Company
14400 Lomitas Avenue
City of Industry, CA 91746

Jack D. Wolfe Co.
2130 Bergen Street
Brooklyn, NY 11232

Hand Tools

Kemper Manufacturing, Inc.
Box 696
Chino, CA 91710

Insulating Materials

Thermal Ceramics
Old Savannah Road
Box 923
Augusta, GA 30903

Kilns

Alpine
A.R.T. Studio Clay Co.
1555 Louis Avenue
Elk Grove Village, IL 02254

Bailey Pottery Equipment Corp.
CPO 1577
Kingston, NY 12401

Geil Kilns
1601 Rosecrans Avenue
Gardena, CA 90249

Paragon Industries
2011 South Town East Blvd.
Mesquite, TX 75149-1122

Skutt Ceramic Products
2618 SE Steele Street
Portland, OR 97202

Unique Kilns
Box 246
Ringoes, NJ 08551

Mike Taylor, *The Everything Box.*
Slab-built, raku fired stoneware, tile, polished
aluminum, lead,
16 x 14 x 14" (40.6 x 35.6 x 35.6 cm).
Photograph: Pat Burt.

Kiln Controls

Kiln Sitter
399 Thor Place
Brea, CA 92621

The Edward Orton Jr. Ceramic
Foundation
6991 Old 3C Highway
Westerville, OH 43081

Lusters, Overglazes

Hanovia Hobby Products
1 West Central Avenue
East Newark, NJ 07029

Med-Mar Metals
Box 6453
Anaheim, CA 92806

Protective Equipment

Art-Safe Inc.
Box 185
Boscobel, WI 53805

Pulmosan Protective Equipment
Willson Safety Products
Box 622
Reading, PA 19603

Ventilation Equipment

Bailey Pottery Equipment Corp.
CPO Box 1577
Kingston, NY 12401

Skutt Ceramic Products
2618 SE Steele Street
Portland, OR 97202

Vent-a-Kiln Corporation
699 Hertel Avenue
Buffalo, NY 14207

Pyrometric Cones, Bars

Bell Research (bars)
157 Virginia Avenue
Chester, WV 26034

The Edward Orton Jr. Ceramic
Foundation (cones)
6991 Old 3C Highway
Westerville, OH 43081

Wheels

AMACO/Brent
4717 West 16th Street
Indianapolis, IN 46222

Creative Industries
5366 Jackson Drive
La Mesa, CA 92042

Shimpo
3500 West Devon Avenue
Lincolnwood, IL 60659

CANADA

Greenbarn Potters Supply
Box 1235, Station A
Surrey, British Columbia
V3S 2B3

Plainsman Clays, Ltd.
Box 1266
Medicine Hat, Alberta
T1A 7M9

Pottery Supply House, Ltd.
Box 192
Oakville, Ontario
L6J 5A2

Sounding Stone
519 Osborne Street
Winnepeg, Manitoba
R3L 2B2

Tucker's Pottery Supplies
Box 344
Stratford, Ontario
N5A 6T3

Temperature Equivalents for Orton Standard Pyrometric Cones

Cone Number	Large Cones		Small Cones	
	60°C	108°F	300°C	540°F
022	585°C	1085°F	630°C	1165°F
021	602	1116	643	1189
020	625	1157	666	1231
019	668	1234	723	1333
018	696	1285	752	1386
017	727	1341	784	1443
016	764	1407	825	1517
015	790	1454	843	1549
014	834	1533	870	1596
013	869	1596	880	1615
012	876	1609	900	1650
011	886	1627	915	1680
†010	887	1629	919	1686
09	915	1679	955	1751
08	945	1733	983	1801
07	973	1783	1008	1846
06	991	1816	1023	1873
05	1031	1888	1062	1944
04	1050	1922	1098	2008
03	1086	1987	1131	2068
02	1101	2014	1148	2098
01	1117	2043	1178	2152
1	1136	2077	1179	2154
2	1142	2088	1185	2165
3	1152	2106	1196	2185
4	1168	2134	1209	2208
5	1177	2151	1221	2230
6	1201	2194	1255	2291
7	1215	2219	1264	2307
8	1236	2257	1300	2372
9	1260	2300	1317	2403
10	1285	2345	1330	2426
11	1294	2361	1336	2437
12	1306	2383	1355	2471
13	1321	2410	——	——
14	1388	2530	——	——
15	1424	2595	——	——

†Iron-free (white) are made in numbers 010 to 3. The Iron-free cones have the same deformation temperatures as the red equivalents when fired at a rate of 60 Centigrade degrees per hour in air.

Notes:
1. The temperature equivalents in this table apply only to Orton Standard Pyrometric Cones, *when heated at the rates indicated, in an air atmosphere.*

2. Temperature equivalents are given in degrees Centigrade (°C.) and the corresponding degrees Fahrenheit (°F.). The rates of heating shown at the head of each column of temperature equivalents were maintained during the last several hundred degrees of temperature rise.

3. The temperature equivalents were determined at the National Bureau of Standards by H. P Beerman (see Journal of the American Ceramic Society, Vol. 39, 1956).

4. The temperature equivalents are not necessarily those at which cones will deform under firing conditions different from those under which the calibrating determinations were made. For more detailed technical data, please write the Orton Foundation.

Conversion Factors:
Centigrade to Fahrenheit N × 9 ÷ 5 + 32:
Fahrenheit to Centigrade N − 32 × 5 ÷ 9.

Courtesy: The Edward Orton Jr. Ceramic Foundation, 6991 Old 3C Highway, P.O. Box 460, Westerville, OH 43081

INDEX TO CONTEMPORARY CERAMIC ARTISTS

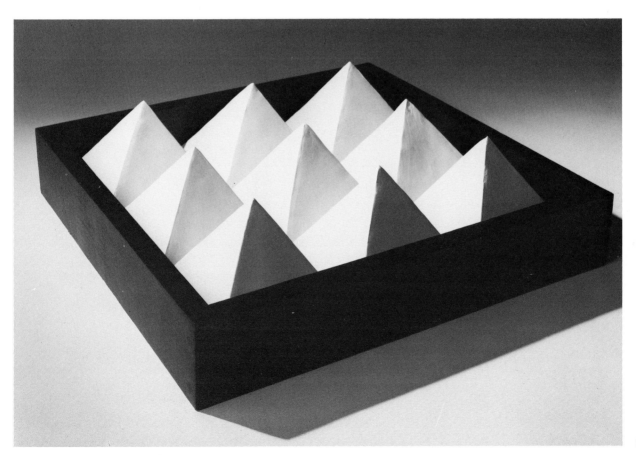

INDEX

absorption calculation, 20
additive techniques, 5, 36
adobe, 24
   stabilizers, 24
   tests for, 24
air bubbles, 21, 69
alkalies, 17–18
alumina hydrate, 140
armature, 111, 114
art haut, 15
asymmetrical balance, 11–12, 40

barium carbonate, 26
barrier cream, 69
Bernini, Gianlorenzo, 146–147
bisque fire, 19, 142–143
   firing sequence, 143
Boccioni, Umberto, 33
Buonarroti, Michelangelo, 147

Caffieri, Jean Jacques, 110
calcium sulfate, 26
casting slip, 22
Cellini, Benvenuto, 147
Cézanne, Paul, 31, 112
china paint, 106–107
   application, 106–107
   firing, 107
chopped nylon fibers, 28
chrome oxide, 28
clay, 9–10, 17–29
   additives, 28–29
   clay bodies, 18, 171
   colored clay, 28–29
   fired clays, 25–27
   kneading, 20–21
   non-fired clays, 22–24
   oil-based clays, 22
   on-site tests, 17
   preparation, 18
   reclaiming clay, 21

self-glazing, 99
self-hardening, 23
clay decoration, 84–87
   excising, 86
   incising, 86
   piercing, 86
   relief decoration, 84–85
   scraping, 87
   sgrafitto, 87
clay sculpture, 15
cobalt, 28
coil building, 40–47
   bases, 41
   controlled drying, 45
   joining, 42
   patch construction, 46
   textures, 43
commissions, 146–157
   contracts, 157
   cost, 153–156
   idea sketches, 150–151
   presentation, 152–153
   public projects, 152–153
   slide bank, 147
   slides, 148–149
composition, principles of, 10–15
   balance, 11–12
   proportion, 12–13
   purpose, 11
   rhythm and movement, 14
   unity, repetition and variety, 14
copper carbonate, 28
Crawford, Thomas, 10
cylinders, 54–55, 72–74

decals, 109
deflocculant, 22, 59
Duchamp, Marcel, 10
earthenware, 17, 20, 25
   iron oxide content, 25
efflorescence, 26

Egyptian paste, 99–100
   color, 100
   firing, 100
   forming, 99
   handling, 100
   Kanthal wire stilts, 100
electric kilns, 135–136
   frontloading, 135
   safety, 135–136
   toploading, 135
elephant ear sponge, 69
emulsified asphalt, 24
engobes, 89
eoliths, 2
Etruscans, 40
expanded mica, 59
extruders, 47, 65

feldspar, 26, 94
figures, sculpting, 116–120
   sectional construction, 118–119
finishes, 88–109
   dyes, 91
   engobes, 89
   flocking, 91
   glitter, 91
   paints, 91
   pâte-sur pâte, 89
   slip, 89
   stains, 90
   underglaze, 90
   washes, 89
firing, 134–145
   bisque firing, 142–143
   glaze firing, 143–144
   firing temperature, 25
   kilns, 135–138
   reduction firing, 144–145
flange, 57, 118
flashing, 125
flocking, 91